Journey to Heaven

Other Books in English by Chiara Lubich

Christian Living Today—Meditations
Diary 1964/65
Fragments of Wisdom
From Scripture to Life
Jesus the Heart of His Message: Unity and Jesus Forsaken
The Love That Comes From God: Reflections on the Family
May They All Be One
On the Holy Journey
Servants of All
Spiritual Writings Volume 1: A Call to Love
Spiritual Writings Volume 2: When Our Love Is Charity
Yes Yes, No No

Chiara Lubich

Journey to Heaven

Spiritual Thoughts to Live

New City Press

Published in the United States by
New City Press, 202 Cardinal Rd., Hyde Park, NY 12538
New City, 4800 Valenzuela St. Sta Mesa, 1016 Manila Philippines
©1997 New City Press

Translated by Julian Stead, O.S.B. from the original Italian
Cercando le Cose di Lassù
© 1992 Città Nuova Editrice

Cover art: Arcabas: *San Luca dipinge la Vergine, Gesù e Giovanni Battista* (detail) Saint-Hugues de Chartreuse; da François Boespflug, *Arcabas*
© Marietti S.p.A., Genova

Cover design by Nick Cianfarani

ISBN 1-56548-093-7
Library of Congress Catalog Number: 97-66731

Scripture quotations are from the New American Bible
©1970, Confraternity of Christian Doctrine, Washington, DC

Printed in Canada

Contents

Foreword 7

Love Everyone; Be the First to Love 13

The Immensity of God 15

Start by Loving Those Most Distant From Us . 18

The Requirements of the Love of Neighbor . . . 21

Doing God's Will, Even If it Takes Heroism . . 24

Casting All Our Cares Upon the Father 27

Renunciation and Love 30

Resist from the Start 33

The Two Pillars 36

A Mother like Mary 40

Be Unsparing of Ourselves
in Communicating the Ideal 43

How to Increase Our Union with God 46

Don't Get On the Wrong Track 49

Our One Guiding Star 52

Just One Word: Love 55

For the Synod 58

Living the Will of God with Total Commitment 61

"Until They Grow Rich" 64

Love and Joy	67
The Joy Which Blooms Out of Obedience	69
Luminous Examples	72
Improve Our Prayer	75
What Is Essential in Our Prayers	78
Look at the Fruits	82
How to Seek the Things That Are Above	85
To Love in Truth	88
To Love in Deed	91
Revive Our Relationships	94
All Yours	97
When Am I Strong?	100
The Penance That Heaven Asks of Us	103
Stay in God's Present Will	106
Announcing the Ideal	109
Carrying Jesus	112
All for the Greater Glory of God	115
The Greatest Pain	118
Not Make Jesus Die	121

Foreword

No one wants to go through life alone, especially the difficult steps along the way. Yet, we do hear of people living very much alone. And our culture even claims some truth to the saying, "Ultimately you die alone." On the one hand these words may wish to justify a rugged individualism, on the other they express skeptisim, perhaps, about ever finding community or the support and enlightenment shared by true friends.

It is to meet this need and desire for community that Chiara Lubich has transmitted the biweekly messages collected in this volume. They were addressed to a network of persons all over the world, who follow the life and spirit of Focolare, the movement she founded.

While her writings reflect her Catholic roots, members also of a great many other Christian churches, of other religions, and people with no formal ties to any faith find in the context of their own traditions and lives ways to share an integral part in her spirituality of unity. All find she has something to say to a world that evermore seeks peaceful solutions to live and to progress as one.

This book is a sequel to earlier similar thoughts printed in *Journey* (1980 to 1984) and *On the Holy Journey* (1984 to 1986).[1] Since the end of 1980, at Chiara's recommendation to the youth of the Movement, the Focolare has

---

1. Chiara Lubich, *Journey* and *On the Holy Journey* (New York: New City Press, 1984 and 1988).

chosen to advance behind the banner of Psalm 84:6, "Happy are those whose hearts are set upon the holy journey." They are people who direct their lives toward God, devoting their energy to responding to the divine call of love. Demanding as it is radical.

The messages in this book are laid down we might say like a railroad track, its path guided on the explanation of gospel sayings applicable to every sector of society. The lives of all on this journey, in both their singular and collective dimension, are like the cars of the train, not isolated but linked to each other in a communion of thoughts, ideas, and objectives.

The author touches on a great variety of themes. She speaks of the example left by those who have completed their earthly journey (pp. 15-16, 50-52, 102). She integrates the most varied walks of life with each other, from the world of economics, to education, politics, and so on. The readings show how many people, as sisters and brothers, have given their lives not only to following Jesus individually but to strive to have him among them according to his promise, "Where two or three are gathered in my name there am I in the midst of them" (Mt 18:20).

To experience this is wonderful. Jesus promised it, and how God must be pleased to inspire and witness the effects of his word in the world today.

To establish and deepen this unity requires us to continually refocus on God's will and love of neighbor: daily, hourly, and especially in suffering, which reminds us of the cross. Pope John Paul II has described our society's lack of appreciation for the experience of suffering in *Evangelium Vitae*: "When the prevailing tendency is to value life only to the extent that it brings pleasure and well-being, suffering seems like an unbearable setback, something from which one must be freed at all costs" (#64). Chiara Lubich liberates us from this deception, showing repeatedly suffering's supreme value for joining us to Christ, and through him to each other and our common goal. She gives us examples of how it is to be gladly accepted as one might accept a surgical operation that will save our life and even the lives of those we love.

We find advice in these pages about how to improve our life of prayer (pp. 77-78) and warnings against being too attached to persons or things or oneself (pp. 87-88). To maintain the most precious of gifts—one's union with God—we need to avoid "imperfections" (p. 48), that is, the indulgence of weaknesses. Chiara calls for unlimited love, widening our vision to the measure of divine love which is willing to give one's life (pp. 87, 90). Live as the Church does, as though it were quite natural to become holy for the sake of God's glory and to win over others to him. This is all implicit in the love of God and neighbor, which is Christ's simple message, referred to so clearly throughout this book. Here spiritual progress becomes visible as a perfect Christian spirit is sought after through and with others. We form a deeper relationship with Christ, a real presence of Jesus develops between us, joy grows in our hearts, and we perform many acts of love for Jesus crucified and forsaken (p. 89).

Will the reader find anything new in these pages? Yes and no.

Mention of the Holy Spirit is not exactly innovative in a book about an orthodox way to live the Christian religion. From the infancy narrative in the Gospels to the Acts of the Apostles, the Spirit is evidently present in the New Testament scriptures. But to treat him as a real, personal presence whose voice can be heard today, might come as a surprise (p. 60).

People unattracted to Christianity as they have met it to date, might find the Christianity of joy, distinctive of these pages, worth considering. Some may never have thought of Christianity that way. After sober reflection they may well agree that an authentic Christianity would have to include this joyful spirit, fruit of the Holy Spirit.

The Way of Mary is an original approach to traditional devotion to Mary: seeing the stages of her life, such as we recall in the mysteries of the rosary, as stages to be retraced in our own lives (pp. 116-24).

Points made here can be both demanding and gentle. "When I am weak, then I am strong," said Paul (2 Cor 12:10). A reminder that we have nothing to fear from our own weakness if we trust in the strength of God (pp. 101-02). Live in the present moment: Don't lose opportunities or postpone good deeds in the expectation of "pie in the sky." Life here and now can bring its rewards, and don't worry about the future nor get hung up over the mistakes or traumas of the past. Give up everything, let go in the interest of loving more.

In short, the reader is bound to find challenging new thoughts here. But not just thoughts. This book is not about a new theory but about a new *life*. It is about new relationships to be developed, and about how to release the creative potential of Christ's words.

There is a strong balance here between Chiara Lubich's powerful push to forge ahead on the holy journey and her uncommon understanding of human souls and the variety of accidents that can happen along the way toward spiritual maturity. Notice how she treats the tests and trials that go with the journey and the temptation that often arises to give up. It is to be met with a strong "No, we cannot turn back!" and with an argument that one can hardly resist, which sheds new light on the way Christ should be followed (p. 85). Pick off temptation in the bud. Have the courage to resume the journey if interrupted. And in case discouragement has to do with a delay too long to be made up, remember the laborers of the eleventh hour (p. 96). This is traditional wisdom, familiar advice. Here is a moving picture of a piece of the

Church alive, following Christ across the ups and downs of contemporary history and personal struggles, onward and upward toward the definitive meeting with him.

One catches here an echo of the Lord's words: "Be perfect as your Father in heaven is perfect," accepted in a communion of mutual caring based on faith with conviction, which soon gets results.

Julian Stead, O.S.B.

Love Everyone; Be the First to Love

This year the whole Focolare will study in depth the theme of living the Word of Life and how it profits us.

With that in view, it will be good for us to pay great attention to this traditional practice of our spirituality; we will be emphasizing it in our conference calls. An international conference call links different groups of the Focolare regularly. Each call provides an opportunity to share news of the life of the Movement. We are fond of this month's Word of Life,[2] because it expresses the way we live our Ideal,[3] a way of life that has renewed our entire lives. It says: "If anyone is in Christ, he is a new creation. The old order has passed away; now all is new!" (2 Cor 5:17). As you notice immediately, it refers to the "new self" (cf. Eph 4:24), planted in us by means of baptism and of adherence to the faith, supplanting the "old self" (cf. Eph 4:22). A "new self" with a new way of looking at things, of acting, and of loving, replacing the old way.

A "new self" we need to keep alive in us always by letting ourselves be invaded with supernatural love. So that this "new self" can live in us freely, it is worthwhile to ask: What is this love made of? What difference is there between that, and the kind of love which even an "old self" can entertain? What are its chief characteristics?

Supernatural love, being a participation in the love existing in God (in fact God himself), differs from human

---

2. The Word of Life is a sentence of scripture, which the members of the Focolare make a special effort to live that month.
3. Meaning the Focolare spirituality, summed up in the Christian's one ideal: God.

love an infinite number of ways, but in two especially: Human love discriminates; it's partial, it loves certain persons — those of one's own blood for example, or the educated, the rich, or beautiful, the respected, healthy, or young . . . a certain race or class of people; but no others, at least not in the same way.

Divine love, however, loves all, is universal.

Those who believe this throughout the earth, are so convinced of it that it would never occur to them they might be excluded from God's love.

The second diffcrence lies in the fact that in human love we generally love because we are loved; even when it is a good kind of love, what one loves in others is an element of oneself. There is always a bit of egoism in human love; or we wait to love until there is some self interest involved. On the contrary, supernatural divine love is gratuitous and loves first. Therefore if, wanting to switch on the flame of supernatural love, we wish to let the "new self" come alive in us, we too have to love everybody, and love first.

Putting it simply, we have to be like Jesus, be Jesus all over again. Jesus died on the cross for everyone: His love was universal. With that death he was the first to love. Therefore what is our aim for the next two weeks? Seize every opportunity to switch on this new kind of love which loves everybody and loves first.

We will each be a new creation (cf. 2 Cor 5:17); we will lay a brick of our own into the building of a new world.

The old world will notice it; meeting Jesus in us, it will find him attractive and will believe in him.

8 January 1987

The Immensity of God

This time I would like to share with you a small experience I had in the last few days.

To take a short break, I watched a documentary about nature. That film actually had a great effect on my soul, unlike other television programs which bring "the world" into the soul and leave a void in one's heart (for this reason we need a lot of prudence when availing ourselves of this most widely used instrument of the mass-media).

Contemplating the immensity of the universe, the extraordinary beauty and power of nature, my mind rose spontaneously to the Creator of it all, to a new sort of understanding of the immensity of God. It made a new and strong impression; I felt like falling on my knees to adore, praise, and glorify God. I felt a great need of this, as if it were my vocation at the moment.

It was as if my eyes had been opened, to understand as never before who it is that we have chosen as our ideal; or rather, who has chosen us. I saw that he is so great, so great, so great, that it seemed impossible that he thinks of us. This impression of God's immensity stuck in my heart for several days. To pray, "Hallowed be thy name," or "Glory be to the Father and to the Son and to the Holy Spirit," is different for me now: It has become a necessity of the heart.

My dear people, Ottorino left us less than three months after Lionello. Both of them have completed their holy journey. The same for Marilen, Aldo, Margrit[4]

---

4. Otttorino Zambon, Lionello Bonfanti, and Marilen Holzhauser were Focolarini, that is, committed members of

and for several other very dear persons in the Focolare. What is their assignment now in heaven — where I trust they now find themselves, through the help also that all of us together have been able to send them?

Their principal occupation (as for all the inhabitants of heaven) is to praise, glorify, and adore God. They see him now, and they cannot do otherwise than let loose all the praise they can.

We are going there too. When people travel they are already thinking of the surroundings that will receive them at their arrival, already preparing themselves for the scenery or the city. We have to do something like that.

Are we going to praise God up there?

Then let's start praising him right now. Let our hearts cry out to him with all our love, joining all the angels and saints and friends in the heavenly Mariapolis[5] who proclaim him: "Holy, holy, holy." From heart and mouth tell him our praises.

We can take advantage of this by reviving some daily prayers which have this purpose. Let's give him glory also with our whole being.

---

the Focolare living in community. Aldo Gadotti and Margrit Hurliman were married Focolarini, sharing the same commitment of the Focolarini but living with their own families. Please note that throughout the book the following terms are used: Focolarino: A member of a men's focolare house; plural: Focolarini (also used to indicate men and women collectively). Focolarina: A member of a women's focolare house; plural: Focolarine.

5. Heavenly Mariapolis. An expression used in the Focolare for heaven, the next life. It is derived from "Mariapolis" (City of Mary), the name given to the Focolare's formation centers and to the customary summer meetings, where the only law required is the New Commandment, mutual charity.

As we know (modeling ourselves on Jesus forsaken,[6] who reduced himself to nothing) the more we empty ourselves, the more we cry out with our lives that God is everything, and that's why we praise him, we glorify him, we adore him.

When we do this, the "old self" dies in us, and out of his death the "new self" comes to life, the new creation. So here is another way to put into practice this month's Word of Life, which speaks precisely of the new creation, of Christ within us. Today, as usual, we have another two weeks to live this, if God grants them.

During the day let us be on the lookout for our many opportunities to adore God and to praise him. Let's do it during our meditation, on a visit to church, or at the holy Mass. Let us praise him beyond nature or in the depth of our hearts. Above all, let us live dead to ourselves and alive to the will of God, to love of our neighbor.

We too must be, as Elizabeth of the Trinity used to say, a "praise of his glory." In this way we shall be anticipating a bit of paradise, and compensating God for the indifference of many hearts living in the world today.

22 January 1987

---

6. The reference is to the crucified Jesus and in particular to the moment when he cried out "My God, my God, why have you forsaken me?" (Mt 27:46).

Start by Loving Those Most Distant From Us

This month's Word of Life shows how greatly God has the love of neighbor at heart. It threatens to bring to justice, in fact, not only those who make themselves guilty of serious wrongs against their own brother or sister, but also those who harbor negative feelings such as anger. "Everyone who grows angry with his brother shall be liable to judgment" (Mt 5:22).

The love of our brother or sister. We come back again to brotherly love. And it is something useful, necessary, and lovely for us to reconsider. As a matter of fact our general purpose, that which makes us a Work of Mary, is the perfecting of charity. The love of our brother or sister. Love felt more and more, deep, perfected, and polished.

At times it would seem hard to turn our hearts to a purer love than what we already hold toward our neighbor: Our heart is still a piece of stone; our love is coarse and superficial and hasty.

But why? Because it is still absorbed with ourselves, with some regard for ourselves. Even if we are not aware of it, we are egoists and proud.

This is evident when we are struck by some harsh spiritual trial (the sort of event that feels like an earthquake uprooting everything, bringing about detachment from ourselves and from our possessions, humiliating us and bringing down our pride), we notice it makes our love for our neighbor become more understanding, deeper, easier, and more spontaneous. That's the way it is. One has to infer from this that the foundation of charity is poverty and humility.

Poverty and humility. How can we reach them and acquire them without having to wait for a spiritual storm? It can be done by fulfilling our Ideal, which can be the means of arriving at total poverty and complete humility, at least for the moment.

The Ideal teaches that in order to love we've got to "live the other person" on the example of the Blessed Trinity. Implicit therein is non-consideration of oneself, total poverty and complete humility.

If we live these principles of our spirituality we will also do well on the present Word of Life.

Let us face our neighbor with an attitude of complete acceptance of their life into ourselves.

Do this in the face of every neighbor.

Speaking of our neighbor, let us ask: Whom should we love first of all? Whom should we love the more? For whom should we have a preference?

The choice in our life has been Jesus forsaken. We ought to prefer people who remind us a bit of his face, because of the situations in which they find themselves: All those who, though Catholics, live separated from the Church; after them, those who in various ways are more or less distant from the truth which is Christ, and finally the nonbelievers.

These are the ones we have got to aim at especially. Are we supposed to take care of our clusters[7] with letters, visits, phone calls? Start from the persons who in some way are the most distant from us.

---

7. On another occasion, the author explained this image, also used by the early Christians, as follows: "We in the Focolare should be grouped in clusters: Each one of us . . . with a group of others . . . so that we will all have greater strength, determination, and zeal to carry on the holy journey and reach sanctity. And each of us should feel responsible for a cluster of our brothers and sisters whom God has entrusted to us; and we should love them, serve them, and help them."

Then we will be living not just with the general purpose of the Focolare: charity, but also with its specific aim, the *ut omnes*,[8] to whose attainment we know we contribute through the four dialogues.[9] I feel that in the last few days I have noticed God urging all of us on toward this goal. That is the reason why I am repeating it in these conversations.

So, how shall we "live our neighbor" in the next two weeks? Revive our love for them, becoming one with them to such an extent that we, so to speak, live their own life. Start with those who appear to be the most distant from our evangelical way of thinking and living, people who are without faith. Start with them. And when we can, line ourselves up on all four fronts. Jesus forsaken is waiting for us there. That is our place. It is for the sake of this activity that our charism descended to earth.

12 February 1987

---

8. An abbreviation of Jesus' words: *ut omnes unum sint* (that all may be one), Jn 17:21. It stands for the Focolare's specific goal: to work together for the fulfilment of Jesus' testament.

9. These are explained by the author as follows: "Dialogue within the Catholic world for the perfecting of that typical mark of the Church which defines it as one; within the Christian world, to contribute to its unification; in the world of the Religions, to enliven their spiritual patrimony and open them to the God of Jesus Christ; in the secular world, collaborating with persons of good will to consolidate, extend, and arouse universal brotherhood." Cf. Chiara Lubich, "The Spirituality of the Focolare Movement and Religious Life," in *Growing Together in Christ*, Jonathan Cotton, O.S.B., ed. (London: New City, 1991), pp. 202-14.

The Requirements of the Love of Neighbor

In our last conference call we spoke again about love of neighbor, under the impulse of this month's Word of Life, and we saw that we need to promote the four dialogues.

For us, love of neighbor is extremely important, of primary importance. We cannot repeat too often: We go to God through that love; we meet God there, by committing ourselves to love of our neighbor we nourish our union with God. Consequently we cannot get good results along our life's holy journey unless we are always aiming at love of our neighbor.

But how do we do it?

We know how, and we looked at it last time too.

We love our neighbor by making ourselves one with them, living their lives in our own and consequently providing them with what they need — become hungry with those who are hungry and give them something to eat, or share their confusion and offer them counsel, share their weakness and offer them courage, and so forth.

Yes, love of neighbor means all of that.

But not just that.

Looking at Jesus we can see how he loved his neighbor by satisfying their hunger, healing them, forgiving them, etc. But he did not stop there. He suffered and offered his life for them, to love them perfectly and completely.

Jesus' behavior must be our light. From it we need to infer that for us too love of neighbor cannot be limited to "becoming one" with them. We must add something else, called suffering. My friends: The life we lead on this earth is of course stamped with joys, with the deep satisfactions derived, for instance, from spreading the kingdom of God, radiating the Ideal. But neither can it be denied that it is stamped also with pain: illnesses, temptations, anxieties, torments, various kinds of poverty, misunderstandings, painful surprises. . . .

These different manifestations of pain, what do they all mean? For what reason does the God who is love permit them? We know they are all faces of Jesus forsaken which we embrace, but often we do not ask ourselves the reason for such suffering. For God however, who makes all things work together for good, every time we are afflicted by them they have a definite purpose. They are prearranged by his will or with his consent, for our purification or for others' benefit, for their conversion for instance or for their spiritual rebirth, or to help them make progress along their way to God.

Yes, there is always a reason for everything.

The Curé of Ars noticed that whenever some great sinner was coming, in need of conversion, he himself, the day before, would have to endure tough battles with Satan, which meant severe suffering.

In our small way, we as well have to remember that you cannot become fathers or mothers of souls without being nailed to the cross. So what do we do?

When members of our Movement are preparing to enter the heavenly Mariapolis, in their long hours of suffering it generally comes to them spontaneously to offer it all for the Focolare, which is very significant to people involved with them. They are faced with the idea that pain has value and must be utilized. We too have to do as much: Reach out to help the people we are entrusted with in any way, or the people encountered at meetings or at Mariapolises; we cannot restrict ourselves to the love of each, one at a time. For their sakes we have to offer Jesus whatever painful experience we suffer. That is the only way our lives will bear fruit.

If we do this, we will have loved in the way Jesus has. And we will have covered another stretch along the holy journey, with real profit.

26 February 1987

Doing God's Will, Even If it Takes Heroism

One of the duties we owe God is to thank him: Always, but there are times when it is particularly called for.

It is what I'm aware of at the moment: I feel an urge to invite you all, bound together on the rope[10] of the holy journey, to thank God in a very special way.

For what reason? Because we at the central headquarters of the Movement have been coming to a greater realization of the enormous grace given us in the Ideal. We have been reading replies, from various zones[11] of the Focolare, to the questionnaire we sent out in preparation for the Synod on the laity.

Their answer to the question, "Why is the call to sanctity not felt by all the laity (in the Church)?" is that the mentality of the great majority does not lend itself to the understanding of, and aspiration to, what sanctity means, or else they have no idea how to reach it as a goal.

Sanctity is not understood because the society they live in, drowned in materialism and secularism, is deprived of true values; in many the tremendous development of technology has created the illusion that man is the master of everything and has no need of the transcendent; and they have no models to follow — the saints the

---

10. An image from mountaineering, when climbers attach themselves in line to the same rope, for mutual security.
11. "Zone" is a term used for a definite territorial area with a headquarters to coordinate the common activities and projects of the Focolare's branches.

laity generally know are people who lived apart from a world they left for a consecrated life.

This has given them the idea that sanctity is the monopoly of an elite. Some even come to think of it as an outmoded idea which at best might have had a certain fascination in the past. Another reason is that they look upon dealing with the human affairs in which life in the world immerses them as completely irreconcilable with the life of the spirit.

Dearly beloved: Reading these observations from a large number of laity, my heart felt great gratitude to God for all he has given us in our charism; I am sure that for you too, all you that have set out on the holy journey, nothing but a hymn of thanksgiving to God can explode from your hearts, for his having enlightened us on the value of sanctity, and above all for having taught us how to reach it.

Do you remember? Back at the beginnings of our Movement it felt like there was a high insurmountable wall blocking my way to sanctity; then all of a sudden an idea, simple like everything that belongs to God, flashed in my mind: There is a way to sanctity good for anyone and open to everyone, suitable for the crowd, for the whole people of God: to do the will of God there where we are, where God has put us: in our family, at the office, in school, in politics.

Here we discovered the connection between life of the spirit and life in the world.

There are many today, very many indeed, who don't know this way yet. Thank God he has given us the Ideal. By its means more than sixty thousand persons are seriously committed to the attainment of sanctity. Many may have reached it already (some of our friends in the heavenly Mariapolis, for example).

Let us give thanks to God and consider it our duty for the next two weeks to walk this road with greater fire, in other words to do the will of God perfectly.

It is not always easy, as we know. There are circumstances in life which make this a very difficult commitment. So let us aim at doing God's will in the present moment, even in an heroic way. This is what sanctity takes, anyhow.

If this is the way we behave, many of our brothers and sisters will come to see us as the models they are looking for; their hearts will feel the attraction of this way to live, and they too will set out on the road to sanctity.

Go for it! Let's live the will of God in the present moment, even if it takes heroism.

12 March 1987

Casting All Our Cares Upon the Father

I trust that in the past two weeks we have all made an effort to put God's will into practice, even in very difficult situations. So I hope there have been some generous and magnanimous acts to offer God.

As you well know, virtues lived any old way are not enough for success in reaching sanctity; they have to be practised in a sublime, heroic way.

And so today I will speak to you about how we put God's will into practice at difficult moments.

You know how our spirituality (our road to sanctity) rests on a point from which all else has flowed: belief in God's love, being conscious that we are not alone; we are not orphans, we have a Father above who loves us.

We meet one way of living this belief when we are worried about something that upsets us. Sometimes it is fear for the future, concerns about health, alarms about suspected dangers, concern for one's family, anxiety regarding some job to be accomplished, uncertainty about how to behave, the shock of bad news. There are a great variety of fears.

Well then, at moments like these, precisely these moments of suspense, God wants us to believe in his love and asks for an act of trust: If we are really Christians, if we are members of the Focolare, he wants us to make good use of these painful situations to prove to him that we do believe in his love, which means we have faith that he is a Father to us and takes thought for us. Cast upon him every care we have. Let him carry them. Scripture says: "Cast all your cares on him because he cares for you"

(1 Pt 5:7). This means in practice, a commentator says, Christians must cast all their worries onto their heavenly Father, the way heavy objects are unloaded onto a beast of burden.[12]

It is a fact that God is the Father and wants the happiness of his children. So they unload every burden onto him. Besides, God is love and wants his children to be love. All these worries, anxieties, and fears block our soul, shut it up in itself, and get in the way of its opening up: toward God by doing his will, and toward our neighbors by making ourselves one with them so as to love them in the right way. In the first days of the Focolare, when the Holy Spirit was teaching us our first steps on the path of love, "casting all our cares on the Father" was an everyday requirement, several times a day too.

Although we were Christians already, we were really coming from a purely human way of life into the supernatural and divine way. We were beginning, that is, to love.

Worries are stumbling blocks to love. So the Holy Spirit had to teach us a way to eliminate them.

He has done it. I remember our saying you cannot hold a hot coal in your hand, you'll get burned if you don't shake it off at once; in the same way we must concentrate on casting every concern onto the Father. I don't remember any worry cast into the Father's heart which he did not take care of.

Dearly beloved: Having faith is not always easy, even having faith in God's love.

But we must try to do it on every occasion, even the most tangled. Time after time, then, we will witness God's intervention. He will not desert us, he will take care of us.

---

12. Cf. Schwank, *Prima lettera di Pietro* (Rome: Città Nuova, 1966), p. 121.

I have heard of many of us being in difficult circumstances. It is especially of them that I am thinking in this conference call. But also of everyone else: What situations everyone has to face in life!

What great need that an Other be thinking of us!

So during the next two weeks let's cast every care on him. It will free us to love. We'll run better on the path of love which, as we know, leads to sanctity.

26 March 1987

Renunciation and Love

What characterizes our crowd listening to conference calls is their goal and desire to arrive at sanctity. In fact this was how our biweekly telephone contact started way back in 1980, it has always been illumined by these intentions; and it must go on that way.

Results? We have had them: Look at the number of us who have reached heaven as small but real saints, as far as we could tell. It is up to us now! To reaching our destination the monthly Word of Life is no small aid, as we have always found, and it is still true today.

The one for April warns us: "After all, you have died! Your life is hidden now with Christ in God" (Col 3:3).

As you can see, it speaks of our spiritual death and of our new life in Christ, reminding us of the reality into which our baptism brought us, whereby Christ was born in us from our own death.

We accepted and decreed this death ourselves when, on the lips of our godparents, we declared three times our renunciation of the devil and his seductions.

People do not like to speak of the devil today, they want to forget about him, they prefer to say he does not exist. However he is around, and just because we renounced him at our baptism we are not exempted from doing our part in renouncing him throughout our lives. We have to repeat our "I renounce him" at all times, so that Jesus can live, grow, and develop within us. Repeat it even now.

We have come to the end of Lent. The next few days we will live through Holy Week. This is the liturgical season when the word "renunciation" finds its own natural climate.

"I renounce." But how do we put our "renouncing" into practice, as we take the road to perfection? Let's hope we are not still in such a state that we have to renounce proposals tendered us by the devil so gross that accepting them would lead to grave sin. All the same, should it still be so, or occasionally so, don't lose heart; do our very best to overcome temptations, beginning again every time.

But I think what we generally have to renounce is less grave; still, it has to be done, because they are things tied up with the world, the realm of the devil often; we have to know how to say no to him. Only this way will there be not too many obstacles to Jesus' growth in us; having him, we will advance along the way to sanctity.

In a world saturated with materialism, consumerism, hedonism, vanities, and violence, we have to be able to renounce, for instance, some television programs which though not exactly evil are ambiguous all the same, useless; renounce superfluous expenses, a dessert we don't need, curiosity, or the appetite for looking about indiscriminately. We have to be able to renounce our temper, and boasting, pride, or talking about ourselves. We will need to deny ourselves slavery to fashion, or luxuries and frivolous reading. Or else the accumulation of more money than we need, unnecessary comforts and conveniences, attachments to persons and things.

Renounce them.

Yes, renounce all of this, and anything else that comes to mind, which ought to be sacrificed or can be.

Renounce it with all generosity.

Don't forget either that the Focolare's charism underscores the ideal way to renounce things (even though it accepts all we have said above): Do it out of love for our neighbor and for each other.

Those who love renounce chiefly Satan, because his kingdom is hate; they renounce possessions, a lot of vain and superfluous things, giving away all they can to benefit others. So for the next two weeks let us live with intensity these two words: renounce and love.

Renounce and love: This is the best way to prepare for Easter's resurrection; with that binomial we will bring about Jesus' rebirth to a new life in us shining forth as Risen. What better way to celebrate the greatest religious holiday of the year?

9 April 1987

Resist from the Start

Last time we were speaking about renouncing and loving, necessary acts for us Christians, so that the "old self" will not be living in us but Jesus.

I would like to speak to you on a different subject today; it is connected with the previous one and very important for everyone aspiring seriously to sanctity.

There is a surprising saying in scripture: "Because thou wast acceptable to God, it was necessary that temptation should prove thee" (Tb 12:13, Douai version).

It mentions temptation, saying plainly that it can not only attack bad people who are on the side of evil but also the good, persons acceptable to God, and loved by him. It even says that for such as them, temptation is "necessary."

Now considering that all of us could be among those who are particularly loved by God, enriched as we are with a charism of his Spirit and sent off on the road to sanctity, we have to conclude temptation is a necessary trial for us too. To be sure, some of us have already undergone severe temptations, though others have not.

For anyone who has already passed through these trials (and we can be assailed with temptations many times in the course of our lives), it can be consoling to know they were really motivated by God's love for us. Those however who have not undergone them yet need to know how to handle them (a good thing for everyone). First and foremost: What do we mean by temptation? Anything which wants to lead us into evil. Traditionally it is said to come to us from the deceitful world that worships idols such as pride, power, or wealth; or it comes from "the flesh," in the biblical sense, stirring up bad thoughts, temptations to impurity, and feelings of anger or resentment. Lastly, temptation can come to us from the devil.

There are also lighter temptations such as gluttony, distractions in prayer, self indulgence, a bit of vainglory, etc. Temptations are permitted by God as a way for us to show him our love and fidelity by overcoming them.

Saints have always met great and small trials; they made good use of them for progress on the road to perfection, instead of stopping still or going backward.

What about us? What is the Focolare members' typical attitude when faced with temptation?

We always try to love: to love God by doing his will and to love our neighbor.

So long as we love, temptation is sure to have a hard time working its way into our soul, because charity, love, produces virtues not vices. But it can happen, it's only human, that we are not always in a loving attitude; that's when a temptation, large or small, can surface more easily.

We have learned that pain, the hardship it brings one who practises the Christian life, is one of many sufferings we can experience, one of many faces of Jesus forsaken. We feel it's our duty then to embrace the pain and conquer it, plunging ourselves at once into living the next moment well.

That is what we must always do.

All the same it is not good to trust solely in our own efforts to overcome these trials. They can repeat themselves, prolong themselves, even make us fall. It is then that we must arm ourselves with patience, and repeat our victories whenever necessary. But we must trust most of all in God, asking him in prayer for his indispensable aid.

Then it is very good and necessary for the conquest of temptations that we keep vigilant watch from the start, as soon as they make an appearance, so as not to let them cross the threshold of our mind. Otherwise the battle is tougher. There is the slogan: "Resist from the start," which for us means embrace Jesus forsaken immediately.

To conclude, even if temptations should be persistent and terrible, let's try not to suffer from them too much, most of all not to despair.

After all, temptation is a useful thing — so we are told by the spiritual masters. It serves to humble us, and consequently to lay a good foundation for the building of our sanctification. It also serves to purify us and to live through a bit of purgatory here below, which we would otherwise have to undergo entirely there beyond.

For the next two weeks let's be attentive to conquering every small or great temptation, and to conquering it quickly. Let our motto be: "Resist from the start."

23 April 1987

The Two Pillars

We are always on the road to achieving our sanctification. Besides, without this objective life would make little sense, because God created us with a call to sanctity. This should be the goal of every human being.

The call to sanctity is truly universal, a fact frequently asserted this year, when the Synod on the laity is being prepared for October.

All should achieve their own perfection. Committed persons reach the finish line on diverse paths. We too have our road. And if we were to ask the intern members of the Focolare[13] what it is, everyone would have their own answer to give: We become saints by doing the will of God; we become saints by loving Jesus forsaken; we become saints by achieving perfect charity.

Rightly understood, each is true.

But what is God's will for us? How does one go about the love of Jesus forsaken? What are charity's dimensions or measure within us?

The will of God for us is to walk a road of collective sanctity. To do this one has to keep two indispensable elements of our spirituality in mind. We cannot become holy unless we keep alive the Risen One within us and the Risen One among us. We are in the midst of the world and, in whatever direction we turn, we find something opposed to Christ and to his mentality. The world

---

13. The people who have committed themselves to living the Focolare spirituality.

breathes the air of consumerism, hedonism, materialism, and secularism everywhere.

How is one to bring God's presence efficiently, constantly, and wider and wider into society today?

How can we defend ourselves from the deceits of the world, ever ready to strike and discourage us? How are we to keep the good resolutions made at moments of grace?

Through her Work, Our Lady has offered us a fabulous possibility, everywhere, in a variety of ways, building small, or not so small communities, whose vocation is to keep Jesus present in its midst.

And so she is asking us not only to conquer personal problems with the embrace of Jesus forsaken, so that the Risen One may live inside us, but also to build unity with our brothers and sisters, so that the Risen One may be also in our midst.

She is well aware that, in a world like ours, it would be hard to make it on our own. And for this reason she "invented" this spirituality which calls itself collective precisely because it is lived by a number of people together.

All of us, for that matter, can testify to a need of this. I still remember our beginnings when we discovered the reality of Jesus in our midst, and it became evident to us that he made a new and very great contribution to our spiritual life. At first, when on our own, we felt all our frailty, the weakness of our inconclusive wills, and doubts about the choices to make for God; we did not understand how one could live the gospel. It's the same today. Where do we feel anew the attractions of the world and of its proposals? Where is it easier to yield in the struggle we need to keep up every day to be Christians and members of the Focolare? Where is it easier for doubts to arise about one's own vocation? There where the presence of Jesus in the midst is wanting, there where we are on our own. And it is logical. "Woe to the solitary man" (Eccl 4:10b), says holy scripture, whereas: "The brother is a better defense than a strong city" (Prv 18:19).

The truth is — as John Chrysostom explains magnificently — "the strength is great which comes from being united ... because charity grows when we stand together as one; and if charity grows, the reality of God necessarily grows (among us)."[14] So the force which emanates from unity is God. It is Jesus in our midst.

To achieve the goal of sanctity successfully, it is essential for us who run the path of unity to have Jesus in our midst. On pain of failure, we must keep reviving his presence in our focolare houses, in our nucleuses, in our units,[15] in our meetings, in our centers, or in our families. And if God's will chooses that we be sent off alone into the world, we have to look for every chance to establish his presence with some other person in the Ideal. Only that way will we have the light, the strength, the peace and the fire indispensable to our complete fulfilment. To reach sanctity we must, through love for Jesus forsaken, keep the Risen One alive both within us and, through the same love, in our midst.

This is what Jesus and Mary have thought up for our sakes. This is the only way we will become saints.

Let us cheer up therefore and straighten out some relationships, if any need to be straightened out.

---

14. John Chrysostom, *Homilies on the Letter to the Hebrews,* PG 63:140.
15. A "focolare house" is a small community of either men or women in which the members are dedicated to maintaining the presence of Jesus in their midst (cf. Mt 18:20) twenty-four hours a day; "nucleuses" and "units" are small groups of people in which members of the Movement who don't live in community meet regularly. For a detailed explanation refer to Zambonini, *Chiara Lubich—A Life for Unity* (London/New York/Manila: New City Press, 1992), 72-78.

It will be the Focolare's gain and consequently the Church's, because — as we all know — it is unity most of all that makes for her progress.

For the next two weeks let's work on making the Risen One shine within us and among us.

14 May 1987

A Mother like Mary

We have arrived at the threshold of the Marian Year, a year in which we want to join our brothers and sisters in the Ideal: the Orthodox, Anglican, Lutheran, Reformed etc., in getting to know Mary better, the mother of Jesus, in order to love her better and honor her appropriately.

From many areas of the Focolare I have been asked what echo the announcement of the Marian Year found in me, and what resolutions I have made for the purpose of living it well.

I replied that knowing we have a whole year ahead of us to be closer to Mary spiritually has brought my soul an air of joy and celebration (we will pray to her more, we will be visiting her shrines and basilicas, and reading encyclicals dedicated to her, we will follow programs of conferences about her, studies and television shows that the Church is preparing, etc.). The reason for this is that a very strong bond exists by now between us and Mary; but also, simply because of our affection toward her. As for resolutions I might have made, I will share one with you; I have already communicated it to the "citizens" of Loppiano and to the participants in two courses being held at the Mariapolis Center in Castelgandolfo.[16]

---

16. Loppiano is one of the Focolare's permanent Mariapolises, that is, small towns where young people, families, priests, and religious from different countries live and work together in an effort to bear witness to a unity that can be achieved among all people. Mariapolis Centers, such as the one at Castel Gandolfo outside of Rome, are meeting centers for members and friends of the Focolare.

It is a resolution I ask all the Work of Mary's intern members reached by this conference call to make.

In a whole year dedicated to Mary, we ought to find the way to honor the mother of God, and the best way.

There are various ways to honor her. One can talk about her, praise her, pray to her, visit her in churches dedicated to her; make paintings and sculptures, sing hymns, decorate her images with flowers. . . .

There are a great many ways of honoring Mary.

But there is one which is the best of all: Imitate her, act as she would on earth, as if her other self. I believe it would be the way to please her most, because it enables her to sort of return to the earth.

This is what we need to aim at, without excluding all the other possibilities we have for honoring Mary.

Imitate her.

But how? What do we imitate in her?

Let's imitate her in what is essential. She is a mother, Jesus' mother and spiritually our mother. From the cross, Jesus gave her to us as such in the person of John. We have to be like her other self, as a mother. In practice we have to state this intention: During the Marian Year I will behave toward every neighbor I meet, or for whom I shall be working, as though I were their mother.

If we do that, we will discover a conversion in ourselves, a revolution, not only because we will find ourselves acting as a mother even to our own mother or father from time to time, but because we will have adopted a particular, specific attitude. A mother is always welcoming, always helpful, always hopeful, and covers up everything. She forgives everything in her son, even if he is a delinquent or a terrorist.

The fact is, a mother's love is very similar to the charity of Christ of which Paul speaks.

If we have the heart of a mother, or to be exact, if we propose to make Mary's heart our own, who stands out as the most perfect model of motherhood, then we shall be ever ready to love others in all circumstances, so that we keep the Risen One living in us. We will play perfectly the part asked of us to keep Jesus, the Risen One, present in our midst.

If we have the heart of this mother, we will love everybody, not just the members of our own Church, but those of others too. Not only Christians, but also Muslims, Buddhists, Hindus, etc., and all people of good will, everyone dwelling on the earth: Because the maternity of Mary is as universal[17] as the Redemption.

Even when she is not loved back, she always loves, and loves everyone.

So here we have our intention for the start of the Marian Year: To live like Mary, as if we were mothers to everyone.

26 May 1987

---

17. Cf. *Dogmatic Constitution on the Church*, 69.

Be Unsparing of Ourselves in Communicating the Ideal

The Marian Year has begun, we have welcomed it with the resolution to live, following Mary's example, like mothers or fathers toward whomever we meet during the day.

Such a resolution, suggested at the last conference call, entered so deeply into the mind of the intern members of the Focolare and has borne such good fruit — as I have been able to observe from your reactions — that the thought of substituting it now with another never occurred to me; rather, it gives rise to the desire to hold onto it, till it becomes a vital part of our lives.

This time, therefore, I would like simply to consider it more deeply with you, casting upon it the light of our new Word of Life: "To each person the manifestation of the Spirit is given for the common good" (1 Cor 12:7).

To be sure, each of us has personal gifts, talents received from grace or at least from nature. God gave them to us for a purpose: for the common good and the building up of the Christian community. If we do not keep them jealously to ourselves, by placing them at the service of others we are putting them to proper use.

Be that as it may, our hearts have, you know, another very special gift in addition to those. It is the great divine charism of this Work of God. You are all partakers in it. It has given life to our Movement in the past and the present, developing it in the past and continuing to develop and sustain it now. It is not a common gift of the Holy Spirit; it is, I think, an extraordinary gift, the type that gets to be lavished upon a person with a special task in the Church, or upon the founders of new religious families or movements.

You all possess it in your hearts as a marvelous gift from God and as a responsibility.

So what kind of attitude have you toward it? You are familiar with the parable of the talents. We must make talents yield their natural fruit, or else they will be taken away and given to others.

The end for which this charism has been given us now is not just for our own spiritual benefit but for others' too. The Spirit gives a charism for the community's sake, for the whole of Christianity. We cannot hold onto it for ourselves alone, for our own sanctification, we have to communicate it to our neighbors. We cannot exempt ourselves from this responsibility. What we undertook at the beginning we must do now as well. That brings us back to the figure and example of the mother. If we have seen that to cover up everything for her child is among the specific qualities of a mother, to hope all things, to believe all things, another of her characteristics is to live for others, never sparing herself.

We must do that too. Never spare ourselves as we give the Ideal liberally to many others everywhere. Seize every opportunity for this, even create them.

Is our own cluster getting rather little attention? Let us do something very special for it in the next two weeks. Are there plans for day meetings, Mariapolises, or Genfests[18]? Take advantage of them to make ourselves available in any way we can serve. Especially in the service of the word. The gift of the Ideal is a gift of prophecy. To communicate it one must make use of speech as well.

We always say that to love we must first make ourselves one in every respect with our neighbor, except for

---

18. Genfests are youth festivals which the Focolare organizes periodically.

sin. This is alright, but I would not like it used as an excuse for avoiding the risk of speaking out. Watch out for confusing true and false prudence, to the point of running aground on a regrettable silence. Of course Jesus made himself one with everybody; he changed water into wine, he multiplied the loaves, he silenced the storm, healed the sick, and raised the dead. At the same time nonetheless, he spoke. And how he spoke! And his words won him love, and hatred too.

It will be the same for us; and that's not a reason to be silent.

Listen well to the inner voice guiding us, and also to the desires of our authorities. We will always be given new possibilities to communicate our gift in season and, as Paul urges, out of season.

So let us keep going on our holy journey, having this as our motto for the next two weeks: Be unsparing of ourselves in communicating the Ideal to many persons.

New life will bloom, even for ourselves. The Risen Christ will shine more splendidly, and there will be an increase of joy in our hearts.

11 June 1987

How to Increase Our Union with God

Last time, reminding ourselves about the great gift — or charism, as the Holy Father calls it, with which the Lord has enriched our souls, we decided we would make it yield as much fruit as we could, not sparing ourselves in communicating it to others.

I hope we have tried to do this and always will. It is a great talent, certainly not to be buried.

But if we analyze this gift well, this Ideal of unity, we see it has two sides and pursues a double end.

It was not given us just so that by sharing it we may achieve unity with our brothers and sisters, but above all so that by living it we may attain union with God.

Union with God.

What point has this union with God reached, in all of us who hear this conference call?

Is it a living reality within our hearts? What intensity or depth has it reached? How is it expressed, how does it show?

We know a variety of ways that God gives birth, growth, and development to union with him.

Charity toward our neighbor is a cause of union with God. Then he makes this union grow through all life's trials borne well.

Furthermore, union with God is developed by means of many kinds of grace he gives our soul. Paul, listing the graces given to him, speaks even of revelations. For us there could have been, and could be now, particular lights, divine impulses given our will to renew our conversion over and over again; it can happen at our meetings, through the strong presence of Jesus in our midst.

All of us now have surely made efforts to love our neighbor; we have all overcome trials and received graces.

The young plant of our union with God, therefore, must have made its appearance in our soul and grown; it could tell us its own story.

Any of us could say, look: From the very first days that I started to live this new life I noticed Someone in the depth of my heart who drew me into unusual recollection I'd never known before.

Another could add: One day I was surprised to feel something inside me urging me to go into a church and immerse myself in spontaneous conversation with Jesus; it restored my soul. You know: After I'd gotten over some occasions for grief, I realized I had acquired a deeper relationship with Jesus through them.

Another perhaps would say, for me prayer is different now than before; despite my distractions, which don't go away, I feel Jesus present when I'm praying and I have the impression that my prayers go straight to his heart.

Another that whereas before I used to pray only to Jesus, now, after many years of "Ideal" life, I'm aware of a relationship also with the Father and with the Holy Spirit.

Even when passing through the midst of the world with its distractions and temptations, another might tell, I feel the interior life is a lot more attractive, to stay at least a little while with the Holy Trinity living inside me.

Whereas, says another, before I could not find any unity between my soul and Mary, now I have found it.

Yes, we could all, all of us could say something about our union with God. We could make a list of its fruits, as we can through unity with our brothers and sisters.

This spiritual legacy is very important and very delicate; we cannot perceive it except with the senses of the soul; for one who lives in the midst of the world it is something out of the ordinary, it has something miraculous about it. It is the reign of God within us.

What we have got to do is not dissipate it, but preserve it instead, store it up, reminding ourselves that it is part of the life we shall live in the beyond.

How does it get dissipated? We know how: through sin, even venial, and through imperfections. We have to be attentive to avoiding everything which is not perfect, as we're passing through this world knowing we don't belong to it, mortifying ourselves therefore in every way we need.

And how does this spiritual patrimony get preserved, stored up, and grow? By action on four fronts: being always geared up to love our brothers and sisters; by overcoming every trial, great and small, through love for Jesus forsaken, embraced always, at once, and with joy; by reminding ourselves with gratitude of the graces God has lavished on us in life; and finally — given that we are speaking of the interior life, our relationship with God — adding fire to fire, which means giving special attention to prayer. In the next few days keep all these duties in mind, and if we wish to concentrate particularly on one, remember the last: grant particular attention to prayer. Let's even make a review of our lives under the aspect of prayer, going from the spontaneous to what we are called to by our particular vocation. Try to pray well, with recollection, not stealing time from prayer; let's even add to it a little. We have so often neglected it or done it badly! Let's see how we can make it up.

If Jesus' presence within us has weakened, he will be invited to reveal himself again, and our union with him will benefit. We will have new joys, new consolations, which will ready us for facing life's holy journey better.

So remember this: pray more and pray better.

25 June 1987

Don't Get On the Wrong Track

Today I am taking up our conference calls again with joy, following the summer break, and after accompanying Norina and Giovanna[19] all the way to the final stage of their holy journey. I would like to reopen the usual telephone conversation with all of you, not so much to comment on a written Word of Life as to reflect on the ones lived with greater intensity by these two sisters of ours.

What stands out in Norina is her love for and adhesion to the will of God. This was the hinge of our spirituality which had the strongest hold on her soul.

Nothing interested her more than doing God's will. By living what God wanted of her she completed the holy journey successfully, leaving very good memories impressed on those who were close to her. We could repeat a lot of expressions she used, many facts of her life, but the gist of it all was to repeat with Jesus, "My food is to do the will of my Father."

In Giovanna however, tested so severely for a great many years by a merciless disease that required various operations and acute suffering, what emerges is faith in God's love (it seems to us that it could be defined heroic in her case). Giovanna believed in this love. It was impressive, the degree to which she believed in it! Her thoughts ran so much on that supernatural plane, where one has a clear view of everything God wants or permits being for our good, that she left those who came to know her stunned, even converted.

---

19. Norina Misani of Milan and Giovanna Carta of Cagliari, Italy, two married Focolarine.

She was always "up," as we say, always on top of every situation and of every trial, and she led others to be the same. She had such conviction that whatever was happening was all love, that she called the acute pangs of pain "God's embrace." I recall the last time I saw her: When I expressed my wish that she get better she answered, "That would seem to me a step backward." By her own choice she was so well acquainted with the tunnel of suffering, through her faith that all of it was truly love, that she wanted to follow no other path.

So she has arrived, we do not know how far or to what great heights. But she left an impression of sanctity achieved. Dearly beloved, this is what Norina and Giovanna tell us today. We would do well to imitate either of them.

But for consonance with the Word of Life for this month: "I am certain that neither death nor life . . . nor any other creature will be able to separate us from the love of God" (Rm 8:38-39), I would like us to take some time over what Giovanna has left as her testament. Her belief in love is typical of us Focolarini. We were born with this faith. We need to feed continually on that faith. We need to believe in God's love when things are going well, but also when they do not go well.

The truth is, one can go through many trials in life. What a lot of people write me too, acquainting me with their tribulations! Well, we shall never repeat often enough: God is behind everything that happens. He has his ends, his purposes. Charles de Foucauld says: "Let's believe . . . let us fear neither men nor things nor demons, and know that nothing can hurt us; everything that happens will be for our greater good, if we are faithful to grace."[20]

---

20. Charles de Foucauld, *Scriptural Meditations on Faith* (New York: New City Press, 1989), p. 54.

Yes, all is for the good. If we could see Giovanna's soul today in paradise, where it seems to us she deserves to be, we would be sure of that. She did not suffer uselessly, she did not believe in vain. Now she has her reward. Therefore it all turned out for her good, besides all the fruit her suffering bore in other souls and in the Work of Mary.

All for the good. So she was on the right track.

Giovanna's life teaches us not to get on the wrong track as we take the long path of the holy journey. We have got to aim at nothing but Jesus forsaken. Make him our first choice. Love him in our own misfortunes and those of others. Believe that the greatest good and the most fruit is hidden in him: "Unless the grain of wheat falls to the earth and dies, it remains just a grain of wheat. But if it dies, it produces much fruit" (Jn 12:24).

Love for the cross is the one condition, therefore, for not remaining unproductive. It is the only means to make the light shine in our face that shone in Giovanna's always, as evidence of the unearthly reality that God is. That is the only way we shall be capable of making a breakthrough into the world for his reign. So let us resolve today to live like Giovanna.

Pains are the seeds of life. We see Jesus forsaken's face in them, and make him our first choice.

And staying on the holy journey, let's be careful not to take the wrong track.

13 August 1987

Our One Guiding Star

Last time, enlightened especially by the example of Giovanna, we decided to be careful not to get on the wrong track, but always to keep alive in our hearts the choice of Jesus forsaken. In the meantime splendid reports keep arriving from some parts of the world about Mariapolises and Mariapolis-vacations,[21] from which it emerges how many people, driven by God's grace and by their own enthusiasm, are choosing Jesus forsaken as the light of their lives.

Then the question arises: Is it an important decision? And is maintaining our fidelity to it easy? For us Jesus forsaken is an indispensable choice.

Indeed we who have been touched by the Focolare's charism feel two calls: to become holy and to win a great many people for God. But to become holy it is necessary to follow The Saint, Jesus, and he has told us in clear tones: "If a man wishes to come after me, he must . . . take up his cross" (Mt 16:24). So there is no other way to become holy.

And also to win people for God it is necessary to do what he did, who suffered and died for them on the cross: "Unless the grain of wheat falls to the earth and dies . . ." (cf. Jn 12:24). So it is also our suffering that can produce those fruits. And so the choice of Jesus forsaken is indispensable for us. We thank God that to us and our

---

21. Mariapolises: Summer meetings of the Focolare for people who follow its life and spirituality; Mariapolis-vacations are similar programs open to a wider spectrum of people.

friends he reveals himself every time in the Focolare's various events and calls us to follow him. Otherwise we would not get the chance to attain our goals. But is it easy to remain faithful to him? Yes, if the trials are small; no, if they are more substantial. In fact, at times it is by no means easy. Or rather, it is pretty hard; it can seem all but impossible.

Here at the central headquarters of the Movement too we very often hear about severe suffering on the part of members of the Focolare, pains that test the limit of endurance, grievous situations humanly absurd. There are harrowing trials that go on for months and years of time, almost without respite, that take one's breath away. It is understandable why people complain and are tempted to rebel. The truth is, pain is contrary to human nature.

So what do we do? Do we advise people to lessen their love for Jesus forsaken, or even to renounce their preference for him, to restore other ideals to their heart, like — if it were possible — happiness procured illicitly and for a small price? No: One must encourage them to remain faithful to Jesus forsaken at any cost; faithful, because he will be the source of true felicity in the end.

Jesus does not wish us to live in nothing but suffering. He speaks also of the fullness of joy. And one reaches it precisely through embracing Jesus forsaken. Remember our discovery so very many years ago, after our first experiences in this connection? We used to say: "It is not true that whoever casts himself onto the arms of the cross finds pain and sorrow; instead, one finds love, finds God."

If that is always valid regarding small trials, it is no less true of the great ones. We get daily evidence of it, for instance from those suffering the pains which often precede entrance into the next life, they radiate paradise around them. So again we must always take courage to remake our choice of him forsaken, every morning repeating: "Because you are forsaken," meaning that he is the motive force of our life.

Moreover it is nothing less than a requirement for our Ideal. This is how we will also reach a positive conclusion to our holy journey, and the Work of Mary will spread.

Let us go ahead this way, because the cross of every day is always a novelty and requires a new commitment to its embrace. Let's go ahead this way.

We will overcome the trials typical of the stage of the Way of Mary[22] in which we find ourselves, and we will be preparing to face the new ones. Yes, because the whole of life can be seen as a long trial, and it does feel rather like that when one is under the lash of pain. But God, who is love, always alternates pain and joy, the Forsaken Christ with the Risen Christ.

So being, let's walk with courage, but with hope too by simply choosing Jesus forsaken and making him our first love, knowing him to be the path to the Risen One.

This is the way we rekindle in our hearts the two most important realities of our spirituality (which is Christianity): the cross and the resurrection.

When that is done all is done.

Remember: In whatever situation we find ourselves, let Jesus forsaken be our one guiding star.

27 August 1987

---

22. That is, the spiritual itinerary for whoever follows the spirituality of unity, inspired by the successive stages of Our Lady's life.

Just One Word: Love

Let us go on with our holy journey, or take it up again with love, courage and hope, in case we had interrupted it. This time I speak to you of something special.

Something is about to happen in the Catholic Church in which the other Christian churches will be certain to have an interest precisely because of its subject. I mean the Synod on the laity, to be held in the Vatican during the month of October. The participants will be cardinals, bishops, some priests and about sixty lay people from the world over, among whom the Holy Father has also chosen me.

And so I shall go, trying to give my whole attention and make my contribution, perhaps only indirectly, to the treatment of such a theme.

As you know, the reality of the laity in the Church needs to be studied. You have all worked to prepare for this Synod, and together we are all expecting much from it for ourselves, since our Movement is prevalently a lay one.

But are the synod fathers and the invited lay persons the only ones who should undertake to find solutions to the vast problems of the lay world? Given the fact that this is a Church event, I think the whole Church should participate one way or another. At least by prayer, as cloistered sisters will do, that the Holy Spirit may send his lights.

For us however prayer is not enough. We are so involved with these problems that we need to do something more. Also because, as I have seen in the preparatory meetings, a lay movement's ideas stimulated in the present century by the Holy Spirit could have considerable influence.

So what must we do? Not all of us can participate materially in the Synod, so we will participate spiritually, by living as perfect laypersons in this period of anticipation, and then throughout October.

Jesus will see our efforts and send the synod members good inspirations.

Perfect laypersons. What distinguishes a perfect layperson? They are distinguished by translating into life that insertion into the Mystical Body of Christ which comes to them in baptism and makes them partake of the priestly, prophetic and royal functions of Christ; functions which the layperson has in common with ecclesiastics and religious.[23]

Let us stress some of their aspects, singling them out in order to live them well in the next two weeks.

Laypersons share in Christ's priestly function by immolating themselves, their own "old self," and letting the "new self" live. In other words, doing everything they can so that the Risen Christ may live in and among them.

They share in Christ's prophetic function by the testimony given as individuals, and by their collective testimony; also by word. They share in Christ's royal function enlivening the world in a Christian way. One way of doing that — according to the Council — is by bringing about a more equitable distribution of goods. How then, for the next two weeks, are we to think of these three ways to share in Christ's functions so that they become easy to live? I would say, concentrate on just one word: love, love your neighbor. The truth is, if we love, the Risen Christ shall be in us and among us.

If we love, we will testify with our lives, and to testify also by word will come to us spontaneously. If we love,

---

23. Cf. *Dogmatic Constitution on the Church*, 10-12.

we will spontaneously increase the communion of goods between us, and with others as well.

Let us proceed this way. Live in love and from love. If this is done, I will feel you all with me at these assizes of the Church, and the Holy Spirit's inspirations will also be accepted in their fullness through our general contribution.

10 September 1987

For the Synod

As you can imagine, these days I am preparing my soul for participation in the Synod.

You know that the Holy Father called me to it because, though every category of persons in the Church (even outside of it too) is present in the Focolare, it is made up predominantly of laypersons.

Our spirituality is in fact very well adapted to the laity (to people not living for instance in monasteries or far from the world in any way); by its nature it is a shield against a worldly spirit that can creep into the kingdom of God. You're aware of this, but let us now review its principal points for the sake of a deeper conviction about it and to draw some conclusion.

We believe in God who is love. This is our spirituality's point of departure. Because of our faith in him as love we are convinced that he lies behind every circumstance in life — joyful, indifferent, or painful — so we feel him very present, even in the turmoil of the society we are living in. Is it not this belief that protects us and makes us feel God close even in the materialistic and secularized climate surrounding us?

For the sake of corresponding to his love, we commit ourselves to fulfilling the will of God perfectly precisely there where we are: in our family, school, work, or on the street. Do we not thereby set ourselves exactly onto the typical way traced out by the Holy Spirit for the laity's sanctification? In order to reach that goal too many prayers and penances are not suited to them, as they have to sanctify themselves by dealing with human things, sanctify themselves in that world which they are called to enliven with the Spirit of Christ.

We don't run away from people, which at one time seemed necessary for living an authentically Christian life; instead, we love every neighbor, seeing Jesus in them. In this way, rather than turn out to be obstacles to our perfection they are a help to it: In fact the more our love for our brothers and sisters grows, the deeper our union with God. Our spirituality is extremely well suited to people living in the world, to the laity therefore. But let us go on.

We live the Word radically. Although the Word is demanding, very often it is the forebearer of God's promises. And through them (like all the extras which come as the hundredfold) can't the laity feel there really is a realm not of this earth, a great boost to their faith?

We have mutual love for each other, we put unity into effect and thus we receive the Risen Christ in our midst.

Christ is the fire for one who lives in this world's cold; he transforms our large and small communities in the world's desert into oases; he makes a living Church out of a few laypersons united in his name. One needs to feel this, because it often feels like we're in the diaspora even in countries evangelized ages ago but now dechristianized.

We are followers of Jesus forsaken. And he is present above all in the world, where laypersons can encounter him under the greatest variety of faces.

All the points of our spirituality, if we think of it, are extremely suitable for laypersons. They seem made specially for them.

Mary for example, the first lay woman, betrothed, married, a mother, a widow, although also a virgin.

And the Holy Spirit. Laypersons are in the state of necessarily having to listen to his voice, because they haven't any superior to express God's will for them.

The same with the other points.

Laypersons can profit enormously from our spirituality. One would even have to call it a typically lay spirituality. What can we deduce from this? A conviction of its extraordinary usefulness, offer it to as wide a circle as possible. In the month of October I shall not be able to transmit the conference call: My commitment to the Synod stands in the way. Quite seven weeks will pass before we hear each other again. Make use of them to deepen the living of a few points of our spirituality and let them shine around us.

In the first week, see how we can strengthen within us, and in others, faith in God as love. In the second, God's will. In the third, love for Jesus in our brethren.

Then emphasize for ourselves and our neighbors, especially for those entrusted to us, the need to improve in mutual love. The next week, help each other to embrace all crosses with love. Let us live, and then get others to live, some words of Jesus', especially those which make evangelical promises. And lastly, listen and help others to listen to the Spirit's voice. So you see, we have something to do.

It is by living this way that we will make a contribution to good results from the Synod. I shall feel you with me, and I shall be with each of you, keeping Jesus in our midst.

24 September 1987

Living the Will of God with Total Commitment

As you know, I am back from the Synod; I took part in it along with 230 of the Church's bishops and cardinals and sixty qualified laity. I have already given a report on this event to the directors of all the Focolare's zones, who are meeting now through November in Rome; all of you will be informed, either here in your usual meetings, or else in your own zones.

Meanwhile, how could I sum it all up for you in a few words? How could I tell you what an extraordinary experience I had, upheld by your prayers?

I could say this: I saw the Holy Spirit bursting into the Church.

The Synod is a new step along the Church's road, where every participant (this time the laity as well) makes their own contribution, offers their own inlay to the mosaic, but where, at a given point, Somebody is acting who is more than the individuals and the whole group, steering everything powerfully to an end foreseen by no one, toward a new stage in the course of its history which the Church is called to live and to pass through. This Somebody is precisely the Holy Spirit. Different themes have been treated by the Synod, and a definite position has been taken on each. One of these themes has been the one regarding the new ecclesial movements, us therefore. That is the one — you can well imagine — which got me the most involved, while everything about the Church interests me (the laity in general, the problem of woman, ministries, parishes, civil and political commitment on the part of Christians, the family, youth, etc.).

There were various interventions about movements, and there is much I could tell about different Fathers' evaluations of these new realities in the Church.

But what is the final judgment, their conclusion? The Coadjutor Archbishop of Bordeaux, Special Secretary of the Synod, expressed it well, it seems to me. In the final press conference he said the pastors have all been "happy to salute in every country, in the East as in the West, North and South, the varied development of movements of spirituality that make the times we live in resemble other epochs in the Church, as when mendicant orders began developing during the thirteenth century in Europe."

The Synod, therefore, has been an important moment for the Movements.

So important in fact that I came home with increased zeal to work for ours, and with a great desire to do all my part — so long as God grants me life and strength — to help the Work of Mary correspond better and better with God's design and the Church's expectations.

For this reason I join all of you again today on the holy journey, following the guidelines given us by what is typical of our charism.

Says the Word of Life for the month: "Those who have, will get more until they grow rich, while those who have not, will lose even the little they have" (Mt 25:29).

But who are "those who have"? Those who make the talents they possess fructify, those who do what is good. We would say those who love, because the one who loves is making a continual donation. And to whoever does good, to whoever loves, more will be given. Whoever loves is destined therefore to pass from riches to riches. We are able to certify this in the Focolare; since its very first moments, when its members committed themselves to love, they've seen the flourishing about them of a work whose branches extend to the ultimate limits of the earth: They've received the hundredfold in every way.

So there's nothing left to do but keep on loving. It is by loving God in his will and loving our neighbor as ourselves that we will be brimful of God's blessings, with spiritual blessings too.

It is by doing this that we will consequently become saints. So let us keep this as our password for the next two weeks: live the will of God with total commitment.

Always live God's will with total commitment in our daily duties. Live it this way when it wears the face of Jesus forsaken, in trials to welcome, temptations to be overcome, bad occasions to be avoided. Live the will of God with total commitment when it is presented as a message of joy, of consolation and of peace. In a word, get just one idea into our hearts: live God's will with total commitment. It is through this "having" system that we will be able to receive more for ourselves and for others. This is the manner to be always "alive" in our spiritual life, to be sure of taking a road to sanctity. Do it, then. Let's start at once.

12 November 1987

"Until They Grow Rich"

"Those who have, will get more until they grow rich" (Mt 25:29).

This is what we are experiencing in this splendid month of November, when we have all the zone directors present here in Rome. A splendid month because the fruits of a year's labor are harvested, a year which for very many has been — what we set out to make it and we want to trust it was — the holiest year of our life. A year therefore in which love for Jesus forsaken got the better of us through the triumph of the Risen Christ within us and among us. A year when love was victorious. Jesus conquered in many hearts. And to those who have Jesus, Jesus has been given. This is the only way to explain the innumerable conversions, the new vocations to every branch of the Work of Mary, the diffusion of the Focolare, and the realization of many projects. It has all grown, and we are happy with each thing. Together we thank Jesus. Even though the many among us who in the last few months have been struck by diseases or been victims of accidents are present in our thoughts, and we want to carry their crosses with them, it cannot be denied that there is a festival air at the Focolare headquarters overflowing with people in an intense rotation of meetings, as perhaps never before. Because the Work of Mary is going ahead on all fronts the Church is profiting and it all adds to God's glory.

We are now outlining the points and drawing up the programs for the new year. In the next few days it will be announced what we will aim at principally, how we can improve, and what aspects to develop.

Of course I shall want to assure myself above all — so the holy journey may be the basic reality of our life — that everybody, beginning with the intern members, is in the reality of the monthly Word of Life: Which means that they have love, because those who have will get more.

Last time we committed ourselves to having more love for God, by fulfilling his will with total commitment.

This time — to have more, so as to also get more — we shall aim anew at that will of God which is specifically ours and is the most authentic way to love God: love of our neighbor. I have often spurred you on to do this. It cannot be otherwise. "Love of our neighbor," says Therese of Lisieux, "is everything on earth; one loves God to the degree that we put it into practice." Yes, that is what we wish to aim at for the next two weeks: to see the face of Jesus in the face of every brother or sister and love him. Know that meeting a brother or sister is like getting close to a mine from which we can extract gold nuggets, because by loving that brother or sister we enrich our own souls. "Those who have (love) will get more." Augustine too is convinced of this, affirming that "through love of his neighbor, the poor man is rich; without love for his neighbor, the rich man is poor."

And so let us get up in the morning with this intention. I want to get rich today, to enrich my soul. If the soul is rich, the body too gets what is good for it.

Let us throw ourselves therefore into loving the brothers and sisters we encounter, one after the other. Let us draw up a plan of encounters. We are "intern members" of the Focolare and there is no lack of persons entrusted to us. Love them with a phone call, a postcard, a gift; with sharing, with telling news, with kindling their inner fire.

When we come to the next conference call the Focolare will have new vitality because having loved we will have been given more love from heaven and we will be in plenty. This is the way we will be able to enrich many and the reign of God will advance. What more do we want? We here are setting off in this direction and I hope you will all join us.

If last year was to be the holiest year of our lives, let this be the year of the greatest fire.

Our brothers and sisters who are suffering will be offering the best fuel to the fire. And it is a raging fire we want! It is a matter of being consistent: We wish to follow Jesus. Did he not say that he came to cast fire on the earth and that his will is that it be kindled?

26 November 1987

Love and Joy

Many delegates of the Focolare will have come back to your zones and begun a brief updating. Others who have yet to arrive stayed here for the Focolarini's meeting. So you will have heard a lot about this splendid Work of God and will be working at it with greater joy. Here at the central headquarters of the Movement we are having a succession of meetings, definitely a reason for rejoicing, such as this one for the Focolarini. You should have seen it! There were twelve hundred in the great hall at Castelgandolfo, all consecrated to God! Why not hope a little joy went up to God himself? One cannot help but think it made the recent feast of the Immaculate Conception a particularly happy one for Our Lady too.

And we felt joy at the constructive meeting held between the Holy Father and the Patriarch of Constantinople Demetrius I on his recent visit to Rome. Joy because at the root of these events a little bit of our charism is at work from the time of Patriarch Athenagoras I. Joy. Yes joy, coming from so many circumstances; joy which, moreover, is a duty too this month, whose Word of Life is, "Rejoice always" (1 Thes 5:16). I have been a bit worried about this conference call, because when it is already time to pass on to another we have not yet pondered the last one much (on the spiritually enriching love of our neighbor), to practice it well. But thinking of the joy we must live with, I suddenly realized it is connected with this love. In fact, our Ideal has always taught us that charity toward our neighbor is a source of joy. I found some small confirmation of this in a couple of expressions I particularly like, from two writers. One says, "Sow joy in your brother's garden and you will see it flowering in your own" (J. Journer). The other: "There is only one way to be happy in life, live for others" (Tolstoy). Then I thought that to live the present Word well it was opportune to continue with loving. Thus it became clear to me that we needed no change of plans. Among the treasures that would abound in our hearts from having loved we would also find joy. "Rejoice always." We must always be happy. In practice we must be ourselves. A few days ago someone asked us if joy and a smile are one of our rules. No, but people have always observed joy to be a distinguishing mark of our Movement's members. Simply because their life is love. So let us keep on loving. And let us keep on in a way appropriate to this year which we wish to be one of fire.

The more ardent our love the greater our joy, and we will have a lot of it to distribute round the world.

Therefore it will be with this binomial, love and joy, that we will prepare best for Christmas.

Jesus came to the world for love, and to communicate his joy to us. He came to the earth for our sakes, to free us from every kind of slavery and from death. Thereby he introduced us into his trinitarian life which is beatitude, joy.

Remember then, "Be joyful always!" Always.

Let no moment pass by without loving and we won't be a single moment without joy.

Let "joy" be, this month, our second name.

            10 December 1987

The Joy Which Blooms Out of Obedience

In the other December conference call we underlined the necessity of being in joy in order to fit ourselves into this month's Word of Life which says, "Be joyful always!" We also saw that the source of joy is love for one's neighbor, which we wished to put into practice with particular commitment in order to prepare ourselves for Christmas, making our own the binomial: "love and joy."

Tomorrow is Christmas, the most heartfelt of Christian feasts, and at the holy Mass commemorating the great event, with the Christmas crib too, the tree, the carols, the presents, we shall be wrapped in a characteristic atmosphere infusing peace and joy; it excites amazement, astonishment, gratitude; it speaks of novelty, the ever new novelty of God becoming man for our sakes. We should like everything to be new, our soul new, even through a good confession, our surroundings new, as one can count on having Christmas decorations, and perhaps by our wearing a new suit of clothes. And for us starting on the holy journey in this year of fire, new for also the way of being joyful and of having joy to offer as incense to the Child Jesus.

A new way. Yes, there is a new way to be happy, which we have never underlined before. I have experienced it very often in my life. It is the way of obedience, of knowing how to obey. You will ask me, What place has obedience in our spirituality? And how does it relate to joy?

In our spirituality obedience holds an important place, above all because it has to contemplate every virtue, being a Christian spirituality.

Also because charity, which unquestionably distinguishes us, leads naturally to obedience.

You know charity is the mother of all the virtues. Well, it is obedience's mother especially.

Catherine of Siena says that obedience and patience "are born of charity ... and chiefly true and perfect obedience." This is understandable: When we love, we obey the person we love, even without adverting to it. We obey God, since precisely out of wanting to love him we commit ourselves to obeying him in his will. We obey our brothers and sisters, since love means precisely identifying oneself with the thoughts, tastes, and desires of others.

This year you will hear a lot about obedience; we want to go into it as a backup to unity. You will hear it described in traditional terms, but also under the special light provided by the new charism given us by God, which makes humanity today particularly appreciate it.

We will learn better how to obey, obeying everything and everybody that reveals God's will, and particularly how to live obedience to perfection within the Focolare, a work of the Church approved by the Church, with directors who tell us how to live according to our own statutes.

What is the result of this obedience, rediscovered, re-understood, and practised? Joy. Joy, it cannot be otherwise. Joy, for with obedience we eliminate our own will, which generates sin in the soul and imperfection, and torment along with them. Whereas in the will of God — a lot of saints tell us — is joy and happiness.

The present we shall give tomorrow to Jesus (whose life on earth began, and was always lived, out of only love and obedience to the Father), will be the intention of perfecting our own obedience. We intern members especially must help our directors to put into practice the eighteen points laid down here at the central headquarters as the Focolare's track for the journey of 1987-88.[24] And so, being obedient without further thought we shall commit ourselves to arriving at perennial joy.

This way one can progress, beautifying the soul with virtues. We model ourselves more and more after Jesus forsaken (in whom we have always admired all the virtues at their highest degree), and after Mary desolate,[25] whom we have defined the monument of virtues.

And so: Merry Christmas, best wishes for a merry Christmas! Best wishes for all good, most of all for holiness, our Movement's typical holiness, distinguished always for its obedience to the Church and so to God.

24 December 1987

---

24. The "eighteen points" is a term that refers to the guidelines established each year to regulate the activities of the Focolare and its various branches and movements.

25. The reference is to Mary at the foot of the cross.

Luminous Examples

We are in the first month of the new year. The Word of Life is an invitation to perfect love, that is, to true love which casts out fear (cf. 1 Jn 4:18).

This would be a good help to our progress in making this year, as we wish it to be, a year of fire.

It's a good opportunity to eliminate all fears from our lives! How many fears there are in everyone's existence: fear of circumstances, of the past, of the future, of illnesses, of death. . . . Every kind of fear.

Fears which we all experience, especially when we are not loving; they vanish in love and for love.

I verified this vividly a couple of times in the last few days. Most of all when I went to Rome to pay homage to Giovanni Zaglio, a Focolarino since our beginnings, over ninety years old who, along with his wife Linda who too is a Focolarina over ninety, gave an exceptional example of supernatural unity for decades, as a result of true love.

His corpse lay on the bed in that room of theirs which felt like a temple consecrated by the presence of Jesus, held always alight in their midst. She stood serenely alongside without shedding a tear, convinced that all that had happened was nothing but the fulfilment of the design of God's love for Giovanni and her, one of the manifestations of God's design for her own person, and consequently the best thing that could have happened to her. And so, free from fear, happy even in the face of the death of the man she had loved night and day for Jesus' sake, with continual tiring service till her spine was so bent over that it needed support. An example it is our duty to set like a light on a bushel basket, like a city on a mountain, so that many may see and learn from it.

A love which keeps one eternally young, so that while Giovanni has left for paradise to meet the God of youth, for her, as by right, the focolare has been opened twenty-four hours a day. The other opportunity I had, and have still, for seeing the true love which casts out fear, is the situation one of our religious of the Secretariate[26] finds himself in; he also has been with us from the earliest days, and is close to the completion of his holy journey.

In him the truth contained in our present Word of Life is evident, and to me, it seems, to an extraordinary degree. His name is Father Giuseppe Savastano, but we have always called him "Micor," for "Misericordia" (Mercy), for his personifying this virtue in an exceptional way. He has always measured other people with a love that knows no limits; he is now measured in the same manner by God.

Though he finds himself in an extreme condition he declares he really has in his heart not only peace but joy, a great joy, intense, persistent and growing, and he doesn't know where it comes from.

Listening to him one gets the impression it is a case of an altogether special grace. A grace connected, he affirms, with Mary, with the Work of Mary, therefore with the charism he has lived with complete fidelity.

Joy filling Father Savastano's heart while he waits for death. Joy. What became of fear? Joy explained by the Word of Life: Perfect charity drives out fear.

So what shall we do who are still on our way?

It's obvious: love without limit, without measure, as these brothers of ours have done and are doing.

---

26. Near the Focolare's headquarters there is a Secretariate for coordinating the life of the religious who belong to the Work of Mary.

Love, then fear will go away. We can never repeat to ourselves too often that we have got to love. Love is God's life. It must be ours as well.

14 January 1988

Improve Our Prayer

We have reached the final days of January. Before this conference call has reached all of our intern members, we will already be in February, a month illumined by the Word: "Whenever you pray, go to your room, close your door, and pray to your Father in private" (Mt 6:6).

It is a good opportunity to take a look at our prayer, at our ways of praying, and possibly to set about improving it. But let us glance at the meaning of prayer for most Christians in general.

A lot of people pray almost exclusively to ask for graces. In moments of worry, of anguish, of need, we turn to God with prayers and supplications, or to reach him we have recourse to our Lady and the saints.

Is this a good way to pray?

It certainly does not exhaust the duty of Christians to pray. For that reason it is judged too self-centered, if it is the only way prayer is practised.

The Christian life really is not just asking; it is also and principally giving.

Indeed with the help of prayer we must give even to God; we must love God in fact.

Knowing only the prayer of petition does not make one an authentic follower of Christ nor a genuine son of the Church. But if such prayer is made in the context of a coherent Christian life, it corresponds to a definite wish of Christ's, who says, "Ask, and you will receive. Seek, and you will find. Knock, and it will be opened to you" (Mt 7:7).

Consequently it is a prayer we are authorized to make, which in fact we practise very often. We use it, besides, to declare that we are powerless and to affirm our confidence in God's omnipotence. Then there are prayers we recite every day, for example in the morning, the evening, or prior to eating; or during holy Mass, the visit to the Blessed Sacrament, and the rosary. They are prayers of praise, of adoration, of thanksgiving, expressing our love, and are made to give God glory. They are prayers recommended in our statutes and rules.

They are known as vocal prayers. The Church advises their use. Sometimes they are not valued as highly as they deserve, because they can become so mechanical that they lose some of their significance. But then it's up to us to refill them with our mind and heart, thinking of what we are saying and loving the one to whom we are speaking. When they are repeated every day they keep alive and present the divine mysteries in which we are immersed as Christians: the incarnation, the redemption, the Holy Trinity, the wonders worked by God in Mary, etc. Very often their recitation opens up glimpses of union with God.

Then there is mental prayer. That's what it is called when God draws the soul into communion with him, experienced mostly in meditation, but during the day too. The spiritual masters advise us, when this kind of prayer occurs, to interrupt vocal prayer (if it is not obligatory) and immerse ourselves in this, called "mental."

I believe all of us have some experience of this type of prayer that is very pleasing to God. We also know the ways to enrich ourselves with it: It's when we love our neighbor in a radical way that we become aware of union with God in our heart; it's in embracing crosses generously that we deepen this communion. In the month of February let us see about improving all these ways of praying. This way we shall nourish our spirit. Catherine of Siena says prayer is like a mother feeding the soul, for in prayer we become more aware of the pain of our own sins, which gives birth to contrition; it's in prayer that good resolutions are made, setting our life in a Christian and ideal direction; it is there that we make the decision to embrace the cross. . . .

As Christians we must improve our prayer, and particularly as members of the Focolare.

Prayer really means a lot to our spirituality. Defined as "raising the soul to God," it is addressed to the stabilization of a relationship with God, a communion. Consequently it is a function of unity. And ours is a spirituality of unity. Let us therefore love prayer and practise it. Along with love for our brothers and sisters and love for the cross, it will reveal itself as another possibility for acquiring deeper union with God. And what should we desire more? Nothing is sweeter or more consoling than being aware of God's loving presence in our heart. Nothing strengthens us more than to feel ourselves loved by him. It is all we need, to make this year into a year of fire.

28 January 1988

What Is Essential in Our Prayers

It may be obvious and even seem unnecessary, but in this conference call I wish to encourage you all, and myself too, to resume our holy journey today with new energy. It is the most intelligent thing we can do, the best thing to aim at, and the most right.

We are being led actually toward a goal which is the start of a new life; so we do not call it "death," but an "encounter," an encounter with Jesus. All have that destiny, no one can escape it.

We are reminded of it by various brothers and sisters who departed recently for the heavenly Mariapolis; and about 150 intern members who are gravely ill (out of our 67,000) keep the thought present to us. We need to plan our existence with a view to the finish line awaiting us; we need to make the only life we have into a voyage, a holy voyage, because besides everything else, Jesus, who is waiting for us, is holy and will ask holiness of us. We know the various ways of reaching this goal. Today I would like to reemphasize the way we spoke about last time. One really becomes holy by keeping in contact with the Saint: Tell me who you go with and I will tell you who you are. But staying in contact with Jesus, with the Holy Trinity, is that typical attitude called prayer, praying.

So then, let's take a look today at our prayer.

We have already considered it in a general way. Now we want to do it in a particular and detailed way.

We know one ought to pray always (cf. Lk 18:1); we know also how to put that into effect. But there are some particular prayers which are our duty at exact times of the day. We cannot examine each one here, prayer by prayer, or make a commentary on every pious practice. It would take too long.

Instead we will stop to consider what seems essential in our prayers, what should be their soul, if we are to be called authentic members of the Focolare.

In the morning, as soon as we wake up we say: "Because you are forsaken" to Jesus. This expresses our intention to choose him as such, and make him our first choice all day long. For us that is essential. Our spirituality cannot be lived without this commitment.

Next we recite other prayers. But the most important thing in the morning is to make an offering of our day to Jesus, so we give every activity and every meeting a motive, a supernatural intention.

At day's end we have the evening prayers. With them, as in the morning, one prays to the Father, to Jesus, to Mary, to our guardian angel. But most important is our examination of conscience: This means reviewing our day, hour by hour, and making a sincere promise to do better the next day, since whoever does not advance regresses.

Every day as well, or very often, we attend the eucharist. This constitutes the summit of every other prayer, the highpoint of the day, the focal point on which all else must converge. A creature's life really is what it is meant to be if it recognizes its Creator and stands before him with the right attitude, adores him therefore, loves him, thanks him, and if it asks his forgiveness of its sins, and invokes him. But it is nearly impossible to do all of that on our own, using the means which we have chosen for ourselves. We are incapable of offering God anything fit to arrive at touching his heart. God is close, but he is also immensely great. Consequently we need something in proportion to him: You don't give a toy to an adult, nor a newborn child a book.

Here we have the eucharistic celebration to give us this undreamed of possibility. What is offered on the altar to the Father by the celebrant (and we can all unite ourselves with him in the offering) is Jesus himself: He is our gift which finds favor with the Father. With him and through him we can love the Father worthily and fittingly, adore him, praise him; ask him for something, thank him, implore him for forgiveness of our sins. Since we are with Jesus, the Father hears us.

Hence the importance of the eucharistic celebration. Assisting at it we must be conscious of this. Together with his, we must not forget to place on the altar our own life too with all it involves: Especially our hard work, our pains, our sufferings, our torments, so that united with those of Jesus they may acquire the greatest value.

Then during the day one prays before meals; this prayer has the significance of offering to God also the act of meeting our bodily needs.

Besides that, one goes to visit Jesus present in the tabernacle of a church. This act is indispensable, it seems to me. If great personalities, even non-catholics, feel it their duty to request an audience with the Holy Father when visiting Rome, recognizing in him a personality on a world level, what ought we to do with Jesus the Man-God present on earth in our churches? The least we can do is make him a daily visit. So the visit to the Blessed Sacrament has the simple meaning of a visit to tell Jesus we understand what he has done for us and for everybody, and that the importance of his presence on earth has not escaped us. Again we also recite the rosary. It is the prayer that links us to Mary, all dedicated to her. We must live this moment well as our daily appointment with our Mother, Queen of the Work of Mary. With the first part of the Hail Mary we too enter into that planetary praise which she prophesied herself at the time she said: "All generations will call me blessed" (cf. Lk 1:48).

Through the second part, with that "pray for us sinners now," we will have ensured her protection every day. While through the "at the hour of our death," Mary will remember us at the conclusion of our existence. Then every day we must make a little bit of meditation where — if we have lived in accord with our Ideal — we can experience mental prayer. The scope of meditation is to put our soul into contact with God, to experience already here below the life of paradise. Meditation's end is to replunge us in the divine and to refortify us.

Morning and evening prayers, prayer before meals, the holy Mass, rosary, a visit, meditation: These are the sacred moments of our day. For the next two weeks let's give full attention to working at improving them, polishing them. Our entire spiritual life will profit, we will make an important contribution to the achievement of our perfection, and we will run more quickly on our holy journey.

11 February 1988

Look at the Fruits

We talk about a holy journey, and encourage each other to go through life as a holy journey, but it might be good once again to explain what we mean and what it seems to us that God thinks of as our holy journey.

We often imagine it this way: As a series of days that we propose to make each more perfect than the other, with a job well done, and study, and rest, and time spent with the family, with gatherings and meetings, sports and recreation, all carried out in order and in peace. That's the way we think of it, we're humanly and instinctively inclined to expect it like this, for life is a continual tension toward order and harmony and health and peace. Perhaps the reason why we imagine it this way is that human life would have been like that if man had not sinned, and that is certainly the way it will be later on, if we so deserve, in the next life.

It's a fact that we do not feed anything into our plans but what is an expression of life, of fullness of life: studies, prayer, work, etc.

We do it this way because all the rest is of course unforeseeable, but also because there is always a hope in the human heart that things will go this way and this way only. In reality our holy journey turns out differently, because God wants it different. And he himself takes care of getting other factors introduced into the program, wished or permitted by him so that our existence may acquire its true meaning and arrive at the end for which it was created. Here belong the physical and spiritual pains, here the sicknesses, here the thousands and thousands of sufferings which speak more of death than of life. Why? Because maybe God wants death? No, on the contrary God loves life, but such a full life, so fertile as we could never have imagined, on account of all our tension toward the good, the positive, and to peace. Next month's Word of Life explains it: "Unless the grain of wheat falls to the earth and dies, it remains just a grain of wheat. But if it dies it produces much fruit" (Jn 12:24).

Unless it dies the grain stays nice and healthy, but alone; if it dies it multiplies.

God wills us to experience a kind of death in the course of our life — or many kinds of death sometimes; that is because for him what the holy journey means is the producing of fruit, of works worthy of him and not just of us simple humans. This is for him the meaning of our life, a life rich, full, superabundant, a life that can be a reflection of his.

So we have to foresee these deaths and dispose ourselves to accept them in the best way.

That choice of Jesus forsaken which we renew every day, that love for him as our first choice, is wise consequently and indispensable — and nothing else than genuine Christianity. It predisposes us, accepting deaths great or small, to make our life a holy journey in correspondence with the mind of God, but also to see everything we had planned exceeded by far, fortified and fertilized.

In the last few days I read a brief treatise on the trials which God sends or permits especially to those who follow him more closely, to one who wants, as we do, to make a holy journey out of life.

They are passive purifications which come from God: sicknesses, the death of persons dear to us, the loss of goods or of reputation, all kinds of problems. They are nights of the senses and nights of the spirit, where body and soul are purified a thousand ways with temptations, spiritual aridities, doubts, a sense of being abandoned by

God; with vacillation in the virtues of faith, hope and charity; they are real anticipations of purgatory if not almost of hell.

What must we do? Give up the holy journey, thinking we can escape a lot of these trials, or at least some, through a more ordinary life, in the way of the world? No, we cannot turn back! But then I listed here only the purifications; we've got to look also at the consolations, the "beatitudes" (cf. Mt 5:3-11) brought to this earth by a life lived as a holy journey. Jesus' death actually calls forth the resurrection, the death of the grain of wheat calls forth "much fruit." "Resurrection" and "much fruit" stand, in a way, for an anticipation of paradise, the fullness of joy, the joy which the world does not know.

And so, let's go forward! — looking beyond every pain. Keep going, rather than stop at that dilemma, that grief, that sickness, that trial. Let us look forward to the harvest we'll receive if we have been able to suffer well, as we are taught by our Ideal.

That is what we shall commit ourselves to in the month of March: Welcome all suffering for love of Jesus forsaken, foreseeing and having a foretaste of the abundant fruit which is at the threshold.

25 February 1988

How to Seek the Things That Are Above

After the March interval, now we resume our conference calls, with the purpose, we know, of sustaining us all on the holy journey.

The light for our path is always the Word of Life. The word lighting our way this month is clear and fascinating: "If then you have been raised with Christ, seek the things that are above" (Col 3:1, RSV).

Paul knows that in spite of our condition of being baptized and therefore raised with Jesus, our presence in the world actually exposes us to a thousand dangers, temptations, and difficulties, which can make us go astray or succumb. So he exhorts us to seek "the things that are above."

What are "the things that are above"? The values which Jesus brought to the earth, for which his followers are distinguished: love, harmony, peace, forgiveness, good manners, purity, honesty, justice, etc.

They are all those virtues and riches the gospel offers us. With them and through them Christians safeguard the reality of being raised up with Christ. Through them they are made immune to the influence of the world, to the concupiscence of the flesh, to the devil.

For us the way to "seek the things that are above" is to live the gospel following our own spirituality.

How? A practical method, that I too have experimented with successfully, is to motivate all our day's various activities with one pivotal point of our spirituality, one of its aspects. Dealing with our brothers and sisters, for example, or working at some job on their behalf, we will think of the duty to "make ourselves one" with everyone, or else we will commit ourselves to loving them as ourselves, or again to seeing Jesus in them. In community life with persons living our same Ideal, we will try to recall what ought to be the measure of our mutual love: readiness to die for each other; or else we will remember the duty which should take precedence over all the others: to establish the presence of Jesus in our midst.

When faced with hard work or pain, difficulties and adversities, our mind will turn to Jesus forsaken to welcome him. In other situations our light can come from the Word of Life for the month, or from our resolution to do God's will in the present moment, or to be another Mary, or to listen to the Spirit's voice, and so on.

Yes, everything we do, our whole life, has to be lit with our Ideal. This way, even living in the midst of the world we keep our heart anchored in heaven, "seeking the things that are above." Thus we shall have a way to avoid the so-called "attachments" one inevitably falls into if the heart is not set on God and his teachings. These can have to do with things, with creatures, with one's self: our own ideas, our health, our time, our rest, studies, work, our relatives, our own consolations or satisfactions . . . all things which, not being God, cannot take the first place in the hearts of people striving for perfection. Reading the lives or thoughts of saints, you see how they fought against all attachments because they practised Jesus' "renounce yourself" (cf. Lk 9:23), a condition for all spiritual progress. John of the Cross says, "Anyone who seeks the enjoyment of something is not keeping himself empty so that God may fill him with his own ineffable delight; consequently he comes back from God the same as he went, for with hands full already, he cannot receive God's gift."[27] We too must fight against attachments,

---

27. John of the Cross, *Pensieri* (Vatican City, 1965), p. 96 (translation ours).

above all by guarding against them with the typical positive attitude of our spirituality. If we really live it, we give our every deed an Ideal motive, God is put in his rightful place. The moment we find something or somebody put into God's place in our heart, we have to detach ourselves immediately.

For example, knowing how much fruit is produced by the Focolare we are thirsty to know of the results of some day meeting, a Mariapolis, or of some other expression of the Work of Mary. But if this is greed to know something not for God's glory but for our own satisfaction, it must be eliminated.

The examples we could give in this field are without number. Consequently, in the next two weeks especially, let us commit ourselves to keeping our hearts free so that God can fill them with the things that are above. Do this by enlightening our every action with the Ideal and detaching ourselves from everything that is not God.

All this makes useful work for our sanctification, the sanctification we must reach at all cost in this life: Here we have the possibility, later we shall have it no more.

14 April 1988

To Love in Truth

In the past two weeks we have lived immersed in our Ideal, animated by our spirituality which, applied in its various aspects, gave every act an ideal motive. This gave new acceleration to the spiritual life of each individual and of each community, as I could verify from messages of many kinds reaching me from the most diverse parts of the world. There has been an increase of joy in our hearts and of the presence of Jesus in our midst, and a multiplication of acts of love for Jesus forsaken. We could see for a fact that the entire Focolare has been recharged with love. Let us give thanks to God and lose no time in going ahead.

If "seeking the things that are above," as April's Word of Life invited us to do, led us to take all of our spirituality into consideration and live it as well as we could, May's Word of Life emphasizes decidedly just one of its aspects. It tells us what our love ought to be like: We ought not to love in words but in deeds and in truth. It's a word therefore which will help us in the days ahead to polish and perfect every relationship with our neighbor.

Love with deeds. We know perfectly well that Christianity is not a matter of chatter or sentimentality, it gets down to works, it is made concrete in deeds. Jesus who fed the hungry, healed the sick, and raised the dead gives us the brightest example. Think of him and it all becomes clear.

But we have got to love also in truth, which means as truth wills it. Love, consequently, as he has taught us. We know three ways especially: We must love knowing that Jesus considers done to him all we do to our neighbor (cf. Mt 25:40); we must love our brothers and sisters as ourselves (cf. Mk 12:31); it is necessary to gauge our love for one another by our readiness to die for one another (cf. Jn 15:13).

I would advise for the next two weeks that we commit ourselves to love in truth, and in particular to see Jesus in everyone. Always supernaturalize, then, our way of seeing.

Get up in the morning conscious and convinced that living this way is possible and right. We can love Jesus in the family members to whom we say good morning, with whom perhaps we say our morning prayers and take our breakfast.

We can love Jesus during the day in our neighbor, who may be a student seated behind a desk in the school where we teach, a customer walking the aisles of the store or standing behind the window of the bank we work in. We can love our neighbors seeing Jesus in them also in a house we sweep or dust, when we wash the dishes or go out shopping. We can love Jesus when we dedicate ourselves to activities for the benefit of the Work of Mary, when writing a letter or making a phone call, when holding one meeting or participating in another, or writing an article, or contributing to the building of one of our little towns. We can love Jesus in our neighbor when we are praying. We always have this fabulous possibility, certain that at every moment he tells us: You have done it to me (cf. Mt 25:40).

Let us commit ourselves to living this way from morning to evening, and not say we know it all already, for we have not put it into practice yet as we should. This is why very often we are not loving in truth. Whereas, if we love this way we shall be working on our perfection, we shall be taking new steps toward sanctity, for sanctity signifies virtue, heroic virtues. And our Ideal points out to us that the way to adorn the soul with virtue is precisely love, charity. Everything in fact can begin with charity.

On the twenty-fifth of this month a nineteenth-century Spanish Carmelite was beatified, Father Francis Palau y Quer. He is a witness to the unique divine truth which appears new in every epoch through the variety of charisms which the Holy Spirit gives to his Church. This father wrote: "Charity is the seed of all the solid, true, heroic, sublime and perfect virtues, just like in the visible order the seed is the principle from which grow the roots, branches, leaves and fruit of the tree."

So he too is of the mind that charity is almost everything in Christianity.

So go ahead! Let us take as our password: to love in truth, which means to love seeing Jesus in everyone. It will be a way of working seriously at our perfection, to accumulate virtue. And why not compete to see who can make the most acts of love in a day?

28 April 1988

To Love in Deed

In the last few days we have tried to love in truth, by seeing Jesus in each neighbor we meet. I am certain that our competition brought a great many acts of love to Jesus which otherwise we might not have made, at least not as many, had we been unaided by the Word of Life for the month: "Let us love in deed and in truth and not merely talk about it" (1 Jn 3:18). We shall aim this time at loving our brother or sister with deeds. Of course, when we were loving in truth, that is seeing Jesus in our brother or sister, we did it not with sentiment only or with compassion only, but concretely. Nonetheless, this time let us make the saying our own: "to love in deed." Jesus wants deeds, he wants charity toward our neighbor in concrete service. He has been our model himself, with the washing of the feet for example. To love with deeds. We know we can do it — as I said last time — all day long: a concrete act for the benefit of one neighbor, then for another or yet another, and so forth. As intern members of the Focolare, engaged in all its activities, we can multiply these concrete deeds.

This whole wonderful Movement of ours is one big work of charity: It reunites families, brings peace, instills joy, converts sinners, saves lives, spreads fire into dulled arid hearts, promotes dialogue where persons of all religions or of good will get closer to the truth. . . .

So at life's end Jesus will give us, for these concrete deeds, a proportionate reward. If even just a glass of water offered him in our neighbor will not go without its reward (cf. Mt 10:42), what will there be for many glasses of water?

All the same, in order to live the Word of the month with greater and wider-ranging commitment, I would suggest something more. In the next two weeks let us attend to a particular aspect of the Work of Mary. Let's not look upon it as only a great spiritual movement committed to cooperation for the realization of unity, or as made up of branches with diverse vocations, but let's see it as giving rise to or sustaining works which are more or less big concrete expressions of love for our neighbor.

I was impressed to learn from our statistics that over two hundred works or activities had flowered spontaneously out of our people in the world, to meet our brothers' and sisters' most various needs. Charitable works for the sick, the old, the unemployed, the handicapped; reception centers for accommodating abandoned or lonely people or foreign students; works for suffering children with problems, for the homeless, for prisoners, for addicts and alcoholics; courses for human development and catechizing; initiatives in the field of economics, labor, and education; services to meet all the needs of developing countries or the after-effects of natural disasters.

I praised God because from the very beginnings of the Focolare the so-called works of mercy have been for us, as the gospel indicated, an indispensable condition for doing well on our final exam, which means bringing life's holy journey to a good end. In this conference call I would like to suggest you give some thought to one of these works, taking it to heart in a special way, interesting yourself in it, helping it grow, promoting it any way you can, feeling yourselves corresponsible for it. It would be good if, in the great tree of the Work of Mary, these activities and concrete services would take on new vigor. Take a look around. There must be activities and concrete services rising out of New Humanity, Youth for a

United World, Young for Unity, the New Families, or the Parish Movements.[28] They are present in your own zone or in others. See how you can make contact, perhaps consulting your leaders. Approach them delicately without disrupting them, simply with a desire to help out — with your prayers, if nothing else.

I know of someone, for example, who set his heart on spending a bit of his time getting more biographies of members of our Movement who have gone to heaven written and published. This way our brothers and sisters with their holy journey completed continue to shine on a lot of people with their example, and goodness is spread abroad. Is it clear then? Love in works, and give a hand to one of them, so that through our concrete love, and through that particular activity, the Lord may repeat, alluding to each of us: "Remember I am coming soon! I bring with me the reward that will be given to each man as his conduct deserves" (Rev 22:12).

12 May 1988

---

28. The reference is to broader movements within the Focolare. Through social projects and various activities especially in favor of the poor, they strive to bring a spirit of unity to the working environment, youth, children, families, and parishes respectively.

Revive Our Relationships

For seven or eight years we have been on life's holy journey, because we want to become saintly for God's glory.

We are doing it because — as Teresa of Avila too has said — we are convinced that all are called to sanctity, no one is excluded, not even us therefore.

Sanctity. Yes, that is our goal.

Sanctity. But what is sanctity? The Church sanctions it in Christians when it can state it has found heroic virtues in them. We too surely put no limit on the virtues we wish to practice, yet when we hear talk about heroic virtues and make a brief retrospective examen of our lives, we cannot deny that we are far short of them.

Which of us looking back can say before God that he has lived with an heroic patience, or with heroic humility, fortitude, obedience, poverty or charity? Despite our good intentions, there are always (and they stay on) defects, imperfections, peccadilloes difficult to eliminate.

With sorrow therefore we come to the conclusion that we are never going to reach sanctity. This situation could discourage us. What are we to think?

First we should be be sure that sanctity as a fact depends more on God than on us. So we should never cease asking him for it as his gift should this doubt of success merely graze us, or still more if we were struck by it as among the greatest sorrows in life, if not perhaps the greatest. Leon Bloy used to say, "There is only one sadness (in life): not to be a saint." Should this occur to us, we ought to see in that great emptiness too: Jesus forsaken. We should welcome him and expect with faith the surprise of finding ourselves totally filled with him. Then remember the laborer of the eleventh hour; he gets the same reward as the one of the first hour; so start all over again in earnest (cf. Mt 20:12).

But how? What does one aim at?

Becoming newly conscious that what counts is God, and that one must love him as he deserves to be loved. Not knowing how much life we have left, we must resolve to live the point in time in front of us by *being the living Ideal*.

There is a page of the gospel which finds a special echo in us and points to what we must do. Jesus says, "You will live in my love if you keep my commandments. . . . *This* is my commandment: love one another" (Jn 15:10 and 12).

Consequently all depends on mutual love.

By living this way one finds out how to be the living Ideal. The last few weeks we committed ourselves to love with deeds. But there are different ways of working.

The great and at the same time simple revolution the Focolare has brought and is bringing the world is precisely this: to live, where deeds are concerned, in accord with the mind of Christ, and no other way. There used to be and there still are many who work, work, work, in an activism not entirely Christian. The admonition of Paul applies to them: "If I give everything I have . . . but have not love, I gain nothing" (1 Cor 13:3).

The Lord has made us the gift of spurring us always to base everything on mutual love: "Above all let your love for one another be constant" (1 Pt 4:8).

"Above all." That is how work acquires value.

And it is to this that I invite you all for the next two weeks. In a fireplace one has to poke the fire now and then so that it doesn't get smothered with ashes; in the great brazier of the Focolare it is necessary from time to time to deliberately revive mutual love among us, *revive our relationships*, lest they become smothered with the ashes of indifference, of apathy, of egoism. This is how we will truly love God and be the living Ideal; we can hope that charity so lived will generate solid virtues in us which, almost without noticing it, will with the grace of God measure up to heroism. In that sort of way we will become saints. Be attentive therefore to this new proposal: revive our relationships; seize every opportunity in the day to make flames of incandescent love issue from our hearts and from those of our brothers and sisters.

This way we will see every expression of our Movement revitalized, revived, rejuvenated, and all of us will become more ardent, more beautiful, more ourselves, as God wills us to be.

26 May 1988

All Yours

One element of our spirituality is *believing in love*, indeed the basic point on which it all rests.

Believing in God who is love, believing in the Father's, the Son's, and the Holy Spirit's love for us.

Believing also in Mary's love for us, a love which is an expression and manifestation of God's love.

The month of May is over, when nature clothed herself festively in the bursting of spring and the splendor of flowers, and started the summer.

In a couple of months the Marian Year will be concluded; it revived our attention, veneration, and love for Mary a little, or a lot. Mary was also, and still is, the theme interesting everyone in our Movement: our Catholic adherents as well as the ones from other Churches, while the hearts of the faithful of other religions and of persons who do not profess any faith were not touched by it for nothing.

So for us the recollection of Mary is something in the air. She has come closer to us. To her from many of our hearts that well-known phrase of the pope is rising, now with much more conviction: "All yours," signifying "All my being belongs to you, for you to give to Jesus." "All yours." It is an expression of love, the expression of love par excellence.

Even one who loves with simple human love can say nothing better to their beloved than: "I am yours."

We have said it to Mary and repeated it. And she has not failed to help us, comfort us, to sweeten our life in its pains, to share the enjoyment of our tranquil hours. In a word: *to show herself our mother.*

But Mary has different ways of telling this to our soul. And for us there are different ways of understanding Mary's maternity.

We know that Mary is mother, that she is mother of us all, but precisely because she is mother of the entire human race (of the people who have passed to the next life, of those alive on our planet today and of those to come), at times one may fail to grasp in its entirety and truth the role of the love she reserves for each of us. Immersed in this immense family of her children we probably imagine that no more than a crumb of her love could be ours, comparable to one little grain among the sands of the sea.

Yet, notice that Mary takes care to clarify the situation and instill in our souls, with a sort of divine touch, an enchanting conviction filling us with strength nobody can ever take away. She tells our heart, "I too am *all yours*. I the omnipotent through grace am here, *all for you*," as if she belonged to no one else and loved no one but us. She makes us forget completely that she is the mother of all the others, so she can come before us as ours only.

It seems to us that only at this moment Mary really enters our soul's house, which welcomes both her and us. An absolutely new attitude toward her comes to life in our heart, totally different from before.

A deep relationship in fact is born: direct, face to face; an unbounded confidence in her wells up; we experience such a strong belief in her love that it feels as if we are so close to her that we can do everything, can obtain every grace. Maybe because we have told her repeatedly, "All yours, I'm all yours," she now replies, "I too am all yours."

Take advantage of the next two weeks to revive faith in Mary's personal love for each of us, opening wide to her the door of our soul.

Since she loves us so much, try to return her love. How? Out of the thousand ways of doing it, the one we prefer is by imitating her.

Let us too then try always to use our life for telling the person we love (God directly: in prayer, or in work, at rest, or to sum it up: in every way we are fulfilling his will): "I am all yours, at your complete disposal, without reservation"; and let us try to tell the same to Jesus in every neighbor we deal with during the day.

We shall all be projected outside of ourselves in love; the "old self" will have no breathing space; we will be Mary, each of us, another her. In brief, we will burn like a fire in this year of fire.

9 June 1988

When Am I Strong?

It is indubitable that an element of the spirituality of unity which cannot be left out, since it is fundamental for our spiritual life and consequently also for a secure holy journey, is Jesus crucified and forsaken.

Jesus forsaken! How much those simple words mean to us! Jesus forsaken is the solution to every problem. He is the key to our union with God at every moment of our life. He opens the way to unity with our neighbor. He is actually the secret of unity.

But I would like to consider with you today another aspect of Jesus crucified and forsaken.

We are pressed to do this by the Word of Life for July: "When I am weak, then am I strong" (2 Cor 12:10).

What does that mean? Haven't we a clear-cut contradiction here? No. It is a Christian law, typically Christian. Jesus explains it to us with his life; with his death most of all.

When did he finish the work which his Father gave him to do? When did he redeem humanity? When did he defeat sin? When he died on the cross, emptied of himself, after crying out: "My God, my God, why have you forsaken me?"

Jesus was stronger precisely when he was weaker.

The Church flourished out of that sacrifice. Early Christians offered up their martyrdom to consolidate her and spread her. Jesus could have given birth to the new people of God with his preaching alone, or with a few more miracles, or some extraordinary gesture. Instead he did not. No, because the Church is God's work, and it is in pain, and only in pain, that God's works flourish.

Several times in the course of our history we have been told authoritatively that our little Movement too (one of the Church's daughters) is a work of God. And we believe it, if for no other reason, because we know we have not done it ourselves, and because we are told the Holy Spirit is at work in it. Now on what can our work base itself and live, if it is a work of God?

If we look at Jesus, it appears evident that it can only find its true support in sacrifice, in pain.

This is the law: When we are weak we are strong. Our Pina de Vettori[29] (she is in the heavenly Mariapolis now) used to say regarding her progressive disease: "It's the kingdom of God that is progressing."

So too do all our people think whom God has visited with pain. They accept it and offer it up: for the Work of Mary and for the Church. But it is certainly unnecessary to wait until we are gravely ill in order to think this way.

All of us have to put up often with all kinds of pain: adversities, painful situations, diseases, deaths, interior trials, misunderstandings, temptations, failures. What is to be done? To be consistent with the Christianity which we have committed ourselves to live radically, we must believe these to be very precious moments for the work we gave our lives to; we must be certain that it is in the strength of them most of all that the Focolare makes progress.

In short: Value pain, great or small, consider it important, unite it to that of Jesus. Particularly value hard work, and the sacrifice entailed by love of neighbor since it is our typical duty; here is where we find our characteristic penance. Should there be no pain, let us choose from time to time some mortification on our own initiative, to be more sure of our work's success.

---

29. A Focolarina from the early days of the Movement, who departed for the heavenly Mariapolis on 15 December 1983.

Hence our proposal for the next few weeks is this: When pain strikes, repeat forcefully in our hearts: "When I am weak then am I strong."

23 June 1988

The Penance That Heaven Asks of Us

We take up our conference call again after a period of rest. We are taking it up to help each other to be, we too when our hour comes, as well prepared for the definitive meeting with Jesus as were some of our very beloved people who were present for our last conference call in June, but are not here today, not at least here on earth, since they have terminated their holy journey: God has called them to himself. In this conference call I shall speak to you about them briefly, to dwell on them properly and at greater length on another occasion. I have heard the summer was for many of us a motive for physical rest, and also for taking off afresh on the ways of the spirit. We have of course all been helped to do this by different means at our disposal. It is what I too tried to do.

Along with a deeper study of our spirituality, I had an opportunity to do some reading on great saints the Church honors, and also to watch some films about them.

One of the stronger impressions I took away was the harsh, very harsh life of penance that some of them lived; they often wore the most uncomfortable hairshirts, practised continual fasts, painful vigils, interminable silences, sleeping on the bare ground or on boards. It was also on the strength of these penances that these saints became what they were. Naturally I asked myself: What about us? What do we do? Don't we too want to become saints?

And immediately, in my soul, I got a clear answer: "You (individually and collectively) must look to Mary. It is she who is your model. About her, who lived in the midst of the world like most of you, not so much is known regarding penances she may have practised as about the sufferings God asked of her through the circumstances of her wonderful, extraordinary but also extremely painful life. Just look at the way she lived them, so well that she became known as the queen of martyrs."

Yes, we must look at Mary.

There is no doubt that for us too suffering has a great place in our life: Just think of all that Jesus forsaken means in our existence.

As a result it is impossible to be afraid of our having missed something. We have pain, pains, and therefore penances. What counts is to live them the way Mary did.

It is certainly not excluded that we too may do some corporal or spiritual penance, especially the ones the Church recommends at certain periods. But in this respect we ought to imitate Mary above all.

I thought back to her who manifested herself as "the Desolate." We recognized her in this aspect as a monument of sanctity, as the saint par excellence, as the personification of all the virtues.

And the desire grew up anew in my heart to relive her under this aspect.

To relive her in the total renunciation of herself (since virtue lies in this), to imitate her in her knowing how to lose everything, everything, even God her own Son.

How can we do this? By living the way we did years ago when we understood her rather profoundly. They were times when the Spirit was emphasizing in a variety of ways how necessary it was that we do not our own will but God's; and how we needed to live it well and live it fully in the present moment of life. But we understood this would not be possible if we did not always give up in the present everything that was not God's will, if we did not abdicate decisively from our own will.

I have tried to live that way again, and I have seen how good it is for the soul; it rejuvenates the soul and renews it. There is nothing old in what God has given us and taught us; our spirituality being evangelical can always, like the gospel, offer cues for new life, in its every expression and at every moment. So with this conference call I am inviting you too to live this way.

Let us pause a moment. Watch the way that time passes. Place ourselves firmly in the present, fulfilling God's will and decisively denying our own, sacrificing everything in our hearts or minds which has nothing to do with the present. It could be some very vivid memory, a deep feeling, an object, a person. . . . Let us apply our heart, mind, and strength just to the will of God. This way we truly love God, with all our heart, mind, and strength: God, our Ideal.

It's a wonderful gymnastic: It is dying every time to always rise again. It is the principal penance that heaven asks of the members of the Work of Mary.

25 August 1988

Stay in God's Present Will

Here we are at a new conference call, to give each other a hand toward becoming holy together, in line with our vocation. As always, and again this time, I must point out and reflect upon one of the points of our spirituality fit for nourishing our soul and moving it toward perfection.

It happened however that the last conference call's thought stimulated such joy in so many, such commitment, and also such enthusiasm — as I could tell from innumerable echoes reaching me from many parts of the world — that I asked myself how opportune and right it would be to propose another now. Would it not be better to keep on living the last, for at least another two weeks, which is: to do the present will of God, cutting out and mortifying our own?

On the other hand, trying to live like you, I myself felt such a strong desire in my heart to stay on the same course; it had brought so much interior joy and such great spiritual fruit; I had no wish to change.

I asked myself why this formula achieved such success? Was it perhaps because it had been suggested to us by Mary, who particularly in her desolation is the typical model of sanctity for us?

Yes, for sure.

But also because — and I found this out in the past few days — this thought about God's will contains our whole Ideal. Moreover it is the task of a mother, Mary, supernatural mother, but still always a mother, to concentrate in one pill all the nourishment her children need.

I saw in fact that by making God's present will ours and forgetting our own we have to believe in God's love, we are sort of constrained to believe in God's love (which is the number one point in our spirituality).

On whom are we really going to cast our cares for the future for example, or other cares to which for the moment we cannot devote ourselves, if not upon the Father?

On the subject of the will of God, obviously it is precisely this way that we truly fulfil it.

So I realized that when we live this way we also love our neighbor as we ought; mutual love is kept alive; and the light of the Risen Christ in our midst is brilliant. As we have to make the pains of the moment immediately our own, I saw Jesus forsaken gets a continual welcome; we take advantage of the graces the eucharist brings our heart; we live Mary (as I explained last time). I realized that we become the living Word, since Jesus, the Word of God, lives in us; and the Holy Spirit is heard better in our heart's depths.

Not only this but also every aspect of our life of love is perfected: We work better; the light of the Ideal shines more intensely from our person and from our community; we pray constantly because we're united to God, and our religious practices are done better; we take better care of our health and of our rest, and of the good order of our surroundings; we resolutely give the proper place to reading and study, and cultivate our communion with everybody with heightened love. Our whole Ideal is contained in this formula, which makes it truly a treasure. So why change? On the contrary, try to live it with more determination than before and more consistently.

I think you'll all agree.

And so let's go ahead: With all our love make a fresh start in God's will, in that ray of the sun which differs for each of us, but always comes from the sun, which means from God. Let us make a fresh start in it in the present, letting go of everything that is not his will. I believe one makes more progress this way than in many others.

We will go ahead like this preparing for the new "Ideal year" beginning in October,[30] a year I seem to foresee is going to be very rich on all fronts, because of the bright symptoms showing themselves, of which I shall inform the leaders of every zone in the world.

The Work of Mary is running well in fact, but it will make more progress the more we let Jesus live in each of us. We will be able to do that if we are always his living will.

8 September 1988

---

30. "Ideal year" is the term that defines a year's cycle of the activities of the Focolare, beginning in October due to its assembly of delegates world-wide.

Announcing the Ideal

In October we begin the new "Ideal year" of 1988-89 which — as we've said already — we foresee is going to be "very rich" in fruit for God's glory.

For this period the plan for the whole Focolare is a topic which concerns us all, and goes back always to Mary: the Way of Mary. It is our spiritual itinerary discovered about twenty-five years ago and explained already. It will be proposed with enrichment from several elements out of experiences made possible during the past two decades: so many, after forty years of life! It is not out of place nor the wrong time to speak some more about Mary. As the Holy Father John Paul II had occasion to say in fact: Though the Marian Year is over, the epoch of Mary is still not concluded; one could think of it lasting at least to the end of the century, when we will be celebrating the two thousandth year from the birth of Jesus.

And so, keeping in mind that the whole Focolare will explore this way of love, I told myself: Would it not be nice to use this year's conference calls for pinpointing one stage after the other, reminding ourselves of the steps we have taken already or still have to make along our holy journey? All for the sake of drawing out some practical directions, or expressing the proper thanks we owe to God for the gifts received, and to have a foretaste of the future, preparing ourselves for the indispensable trials to come?

For this reason I would like today to submit to your attention and mine the first stage of the Way of Mary: the annunciation. For us it stands for the announcement of the Ideal, that moment in our life when God manifested himself to us in a special way with a higher light; he called us, he chose us for a definite end of his own, and we responded to him, making him the reason for living.

This way we found ourselves launched upon a new life, on a divine adventure, where we have tried to love him, living the spirituality he gave us.

As we rethink that instant today I would like us to stop for a moment, to recollect ourselves in the depth of our hearts, and ask ourselves again with amazement: God chose me! But who is he, who chose me?

Raising our minds from all that occupies us in this world (our business, home, or family, the news of the day . . .), we could go back in thought to the summer, when we could contemplate perhaps an endless stretch of sea, a high mountain chain, an impressive glacier or the vault of the sky dotted with stars. What majesty! The immensity of it!

And through the dazzling splendor of nature, we would climb back to its author: God, the king of the universe, the Lord of the galaxies, the Infinite.

We would repeat to ourselves: He is the one who looked at me one day and called me.

Then, if the perception of his majesty flattened us, the certainty that he has chosen us could open our heart, arousing a longing to discover and find, behind such glorious beauty in creation, his face and his presence.

God is here. For he is everywhere, he's beneath the glittering of a stream, inside the opening of a flower, in a bright dawn sky or the red sunset, and on top of a snowcovered peak. Then we know that after becoming man he has become present in certain places in a special way: in tabernacles, at the core of our soul, in each brother and sister, above all in one who suffers more; he is in our midst if we love one another; he is in the Church and its pastors; in his Word, in his will, where we have tried to love him at all times and shall keep on in the next few days.

All the same it would be my wish and my advice that in these two weeks ahead of us we seek him especially where nature reveals him to us.

It is true that following the period of our summer we went back to work in our cement metropolises, built by the hand of man in the midst of the noise of the world, where nature is rarely preserved. All the same, if we want, a bit of blue sky glimpsed between the peaks of skyscrapers is enough to remind us of God; a ray of sunlight, which does not fail to pierce even through the bars of a prison, is enough; a flower, a meadow, a child's face is enough.

And I wish we would respond to his love for us, so special, declaring our total love for him; adoring him, prostrate on the ground, at least spiritually; praising him with the best music that rises from our hearts; glorifying him with our whole life. We must do this: Love God for his own sake in his immensity, in his infinity, in his beauty, in his splendor, and in his omnipotence.

That will help us return into the midst of humanity, which is where we belong, restored as Jesus certainly was when he had prayed to the Father under the starry sky all night on the mountains, and returned among people to do some good.

So let us live our own annunciation in these coming days, like Mary welcoming God in our heart, whom we would like to rediscover present everywhere in nature. Let God enter into us to a greater degree with his graces, with the charism for which he destined us, so that, as already in Mary, his design for us may be completed.

To conclude: live the present letting go of everything, but stopping now and then to adore the God who has called us.

22 September 1988

Carrying Jesus

Last time, intending to run through the stages of the Way of Mary again, at least in some of its aspects, we reflected on the annunciation and wished to answer the question of who has called us, who has chosen us to walk on this his road of unity. Freshly surprised, profoundly grateful, and utterly amazed, we have reconfirmed that it is God, Lord of creation. We now pass on to the second stage of the Way of Mary, which recalls another episode in Our Lady's life.

Immediately after the annunciation — "in those days," says Luke (cf. Lk 1:39) — she set out on a journey, to go to help Elizabeth, since she as well was expecting a baby though in her late age. Mary went there "in haste" says the gospel, carrying Jesus in her. And as soon as she had greeted Elizabeth, the baby leapt for joy in Elizabeth's womb.

The analogy between this episode in Mary's life, however extraordinary, and what, after our own annunciation, we too are impelled to do, is clear.

As soon as one has come to know God's love, in a totally new way, the first thing a member of the Focolare does is set himself to love. He does it immediately, "in haste," without interspersing delays. It is similar in every case. Our charism makes us behave this way. It does not move us so much into the adoration of God or into contemplation (even though our heart is filled with it) but... one goes. One goes because the Holy Spirit impels us in that direction. One goes in haste because — as has been written — "the Holy Spirit does not permit delays."

We go to love and "make ourself one" with those near to us, to provide our service. In another way we too carry Jesus within us, in our hearts, because, since we love, the "new self" lives in us, Jesus lives. And what first affects the persons we meet is Jesus in us, a little like he whom Mary was carrying in her womb made Elizabeth's baby leap up.

This going to love is one of the novelties the Focolare brought. I remember that when we were starting out, at least in the place where we lived, one thought of charity as if it were nothing but almsgiving, generosity, financial aid, which took away its fascination.

The Ideal cooperated in the rekindling of the fire of love. Then, after having carried Jesus in us by loving, one must go on to concrete service. Mary spent three months aiding her cousin in all the housework. And that's what we must do: Love is incomplete if it is not concrete.

Mary therefore, also in her second episode, manifests herself as our model, as our way. We now understand that the Holy Spirit began to mould within us, from the very start of our new life, the figure of Mary.

What shall we put into practice, accordingly, in the next two weeks?

As real "little Mary's" remember who are the neighbors we owe a debt of love: They are all the ones we live with, those we meet during the day, the persons in our cluster, the participants in our meetings, the various brothers and sisters we know especially through our activities, and in whom we find Jesus forsaken.

Let us go with haste toward as many as we can, loving them, and offering them what they need or desire: aid, advice, understanding, compassion, interest, money, clothing. Providence will help us as it helped the first Focolarine and as it is always helping.

So first carry Jesus in our hearts with love and then offer all we can.

Jesus will tell us: "You have done it to me" (cf. Mt 25:40). This is how he will confirm that the proper way to love him is precisely to love our brothers and sisters.

13 October 1988

All for the Greater Glory of God

As you all know, we thought that for our conference calls these months we would consider the stages of the Way of Mary; not so much what is central to them (which will be treated in the theme for the year) as some of their particulars. Lately, as I was doing some meditating on the third stage of the Way of Mary (the birth of Jesus), I paused over the first words the angels sang on that extraordinary occasion: "Glory to God in the highest" (Lk 2:14).

Especially of late, we have been committing ourselves to the glorification of God, above all in the splendors of nature. Today, as we meditate this third mystery in Mary's life, let's learn from the angels to glorify God for the presence of Jesus on earth.

We have lots of occasions to glorify God on this account: in the face of every tabernacle, for example, and in all the other ways he is present on earth.

But at this moment I think we ought to consider one kind of presence in particular.

It is that of Jesus in the Work of Mary, the Focolare, which is God's work.

You know how Christmas, Jesus' birth, always leads us to think of Jesus in our midst, of his birth and rebirth among us all over the world through our mutual love.

Well then, this Jesus, so true, so alive, though present only spiritually, has to be glorified.

But do we do it? Do we glorify him enough?

Our membership in the Focolare certainly gives us continual opportunities for it, but we don't always notice them. That is not good, since just as our heart needs to love God so it also needs to give him glory — whereas it can happen, sometimes, that we don't know how.

Well then, we must understand that the Focolare's very way of life is all glory to God, or rather it can be all glory to God. For example, when we tell of our Movement's extraordinary expansion, seeing it as a logical result of God's working (since anyway it could not be simply a product of human effort), aren't we raising great glory to God?

And is that not a good thing to do? Done at the right moment it is very good, it is evangelical. Jesus says: "That men may see your good works and glorify the Father" (cf. Mt 5:16). When we tell of our personal or collective experiences in which we trace a divine golden thread—the action of God in each of us and in us as a group—have we not perhaps yet another concrete opportunity to give glory to God?

And when we write each other or tell with joyful hearts our impressions, the fruits, the effects on us or on other persons of a talk, a day of retreat, or of an event within the Work of Mary, is this not yet again perhaps a way of glorifying God?

What is important, indispensable even, is that it always be God who is glorified in his work and not ourselves, people, or other things. Even though the works seem to belong to somebody, they are really God's. Our contribution is there, but it is always that of a useless and unfaithful servant.

However there are within the Work of Mary other great opportunities too for glorifying God. We have to take them.

We completely agree with Mother Teresa of Calcutta's thought about this, when she says that if God has performed a work, then that is a truth which must be preached, because Christ is the truth and Christ must be preached.

Let us accordingly be happy, extremely happy: The Lord, in the third stage of the Way of Mary, gives us a new impulse on our holy journey.

Where there is Jesus (and he is also among us in the Work of Mary), we have to sing his glory. And we have to do it with deeds, with words, with writing, with mimes and songs, with the means of communication, etc.

It is the intention we shall have in all the activities in the Focolare during the next two weeks: all for his glory, all for the greater glory of God.

27 October 1988

The Greatest Pain

Today, following the pause while you were being updated about the month of October spent by the zone directors in Rome and about the program for the new "Ideal year" of 1988-89, here we are again, sharing some helpful thoughts for our holy journey. The last few times, under a few aspects at least, we considered more deeply those first three stages along the Way of Mary. We are now at the fourth. We know what it means: Mary, with Joseph, presents the baby Jesus in the temple and the aged Simeon foretells to her that a sword will pierce her soul. It is an episode, this, which makes you think: Why on earth did God wish Mary to receive an anticipated announcement of the cross? Why on earth a prophecy which could embitter her whole life?

Because Mary had to be the first one of all to live the Christian vocation: the call to love. And on this earth no one can live a life of love, the life of true love, without knowing pain. For the Christian, indeed, to love means to live not one's own but God's will, and that costs; not to live ourselves, but our brothers and sisters, which means denying ourselves, sacrificing ourselves, dying, making the old self perish, letting the new self live, even though love then becomes a foreboding of new light, of true peace, of complete joy.

This is the reason why to all of us too, great or small, one day the fourth stage of the Way of Mary was presented, when Jesus forsaken was announced to us. He is in fact the sole condition for walking that road of love which struck us like lightning and attracted us.

We came to know the fourth stage of the Way of Mary (though from time to time it comes back again into our life) when through the deeper study of our spirituality, or through a painful situation, or at the voice of the Holy Spirit within us, or some other way, we were invited to choose him again, Jesus forsaken, in personal suffering, in the practice of virtues, in brothers and sisters who resemble him the more, or in the specific goals[31] of the Work of Mary.

This is the fourth stage. We wish to relive it also today, precisely in that light and in that way that we learned it from the Focolare.

In fact, in the Focolare we do not want to simply embrace the cross, each of life's crosses, in a general way. Driven by love for Jesus, we decided we would follow him into his greatest pain. Aware that we have only one life, we took that decision. But what is the result of such a choice for our life? We have to be ever ready to welcome and to suffer, for him and with him, even the greatest pains. Yes: the greatest pains. For us this is what it means to have chosen Jesus forsaken. We may not perhaps have thought enough in our life about the commitment we made; we might have minimized it, toned it down. We have even perhaps exploited Jesus forsaken as a means for peace and joy. Consequently he has not been able to produce those extraordinary fruits in us which can be expected from him. So what is to be done?

Let the review of the fourth stage of the Way of Mary be for us all, in the next two weeks, the chance to get ourselves into the right dispositions before God.

Each day has its cross. That is how it will be for us too. Let's commit ourselves to welcoming Jesus forsaken in it

---

31. A reference to the various dialogues the Focolare is active in: ecumenical, interreligious, and with people whose values do not embrace a particular faith.

with open hearts, not telling him just, "I love you, I want you," but also, "What you are giving me is still small, because I am called to more with your grace."

This way we shall really love him, in accord with our vocation. We have said this new year can have a title: a most fruitful year.

That will come about above all if we each have a new conversion: conversion to him forsaken, in his greatest pain. This may be an appalling decision. But it will make us learn here below already the deepest ineffable joys of union with God and the wonders of unity among people.

8 December 1988

Not Make Jesus Die

There are few days left now till Christmas. This is the occasion to put holiday clothes on again, for a new rebirth in our Ideal. What will bring us to this rebirth is the study of the next stage in the Way of Mary: the flight into Egypt.

Last time we were talking about Jesus forsaken, of the greatest pain. The cross is in fact the condition for walking safely along our road: the road of love.

This time we take into consideration the first episode the gospel describes, when Mary with Joseph had to face and overcome a true cross: Herod is after the baby Jesus to murder him; but an angel warns Joseph in a dream and he flees into Egypt with the family.

So Mary is in danger of losing Jesus. So little, yet already under threat for his life.

To escape this terrible danger, Mary along with Joseph faces the discomforts of a long journey.

The danger of losing Jesus, of making Jesus die.

Our Ideal has made Jesus live fully in our hearts. He accomplished this by kindling love there. Look how the Risen One has appeared through the death of our old self, with a long procession of gifts for the joy of our soul and the building up of the reign of God in the world.

But we have got to keep this love alight, this true love, and drive away everything that might put it out, everything capable, in a way, of making Jesus die inside us.

Keep that love burning, the love the Holy Spirit has poured forth in our hearts, which, as we saw a while ago, has to be expressed in concrete action.

In the next two weeks we must examine ourselves precisely on this particular of love, on its concreteness, and work at making it authentic.

How?

One opportunity is afforded by a theme of our current year, which speaks of poverty, of the poverty which for us means especially a result of charity put into practice. This month's Word of Life provides another opportunity: "Let the man who has two coats give to him who has none" (Lk 3:11). We know how easy it is, living in the world, to gradually accumulate objects which are useful more or less, or superfluous, and keep them at home.

It could be an extra pen, book, dress, tool, picture, or carpet; linen or furniture; bulky or little things, a sum of money. . . . Why not collect all these objects and put them at the disposal of people in our community who don't have any, or for the poor, or for meeting the "daily Jesus forsaken" as we call the calamities which cast so many into pain, into distress, into the cold or into danger?

Every morning we wash our face when we get up. Wouldn't we need perhaps every year, at the first of the year, to check out our surplus and give it away out of the obligation of charity? I've said this before to the Focolarini. In the focolare from time to time we do what we call "making the bundle": piling up all the things that aren't needed any more and distributing them. Couldn't this be practised by all of us who are intern members of the Focolare?

If we collect our surplus and give it away, our charity toward our neighbor shall be real; that way we shall preserve the living presence in us of the Risen One.

My experience has been that to put this into practice one needs a little time. You have to think carefully of each object at a time. Dispose of course only of those things which we can call our own, and define that this one is superfluous that one not. And be generous, realizing that it is better to do without something useful than to have more than you need.

The flight into Egypt. Mary fled so that Jesus would not have his life taken. Let us flee too, from those attachments, from that large or little bit of consumerism that, however involuntarily, has infiltrated our lives.

We will feel freer and lighter, better disposed to do the Work of God and to make of this a very fruitful year.

22 December 1988

Other Books by Chiara Lubich

CHRISTIAN LIVING TODAY
Meditations
by Chiara Lubich   **7th printing**

"Like shafts of sunlight that break through the clouds on a dreary day, these meditations touch us and turn our most mundane activities into brightly lit God-moments."

  Liguorian

    ISBN 1-56548-094-5, paper 5 1/8 x 8, 134 pp., $9.95

A CALL TO LOVE
Spiritual Writings, v. 1
by Chiara Lubich   **2d Printing**

"Chiara Lubich has established herself as a Christian writer of considerable proportions. Given her prolific literary output it is fitting that New City Press should issue a retrospective series of Lubich's best works, titled Spiritual Writings. The first work in this series *A Call to Love* comprises three of her most popular studies of momentous Christian living: *Our Yes to God* (1980), *The Word of Life* (1974), and *The Eucharist* (1977)."

  B.C. Catholic

    ISBN 1-56548-077-5, 5 1/8 x 8, 180 pp., $9.95

MAY THEY ALL BE ONE
by Chiara Lubich   **6th printing**

Chiara tells her story and that of the Focolare Movement. The perfect book for those who wish to know more about the Focolare and the spirituality of unity.

    ISBN 0-911782-46-X, paper, 4 1/2 x 7, 188 pp., $5.95

THE LOVE THAT COMES FROM GOD
Reflections on the Family
by Chiara Lubich

"I see this work as truly helpful, especially strong on viewing family through the lens of faith. I will be glad to use it and recommend it."

  Sr. Barbara Markey,
  Director of the Omaha Family Life Office
  Author of FOCCUS *Marriage Preparation*

    ISBN 1-56548-030-9, 5 1/8 x 8, 96 pp., $6.95

To order call 1-800-462-5980